Comprehensive Ruby Programming

Go from beginner to confident programmer

Jordan Hudgens

BIRMINGHAM - MUMBAI

Comprehensive Ruby Programming

First published: June 2017

Production reference: 1280617

Published by Packt Publishing Ltd.
Livery Place
35 Livery Street
Birmingham
B3 2PB, UK.

ISBN 978-1-78728-064-9

Credits

Author
Jordan Hudgens

Copy Editor
Tom Jacob

Project Coordinator
Suzanne Coutinho

Proofreader
Safis Editing

Acquisition Editor
Ben Renow-Clarke

Indexer
Aishwarya Gangawane

Content Development Editor
Radhika Atitkar

Graphics
Kirk D'Penha

Technical Editor
Bhagyashree Rai

Production Coordinator
Arvindkumar Gupta

About the Author

Jordan Hudgens is the CTO and founder of DevCamp, where he leads instruction and curriculum development for all the DevCamp and Bottega code schools around the US.

As a developer over the past decade, Jordan has traveled the world building applications and training individuals on a wide variety of topics, including Ruby development, big data analysis, and software engineering.

Jordan focuses on project-driven education as opposed to theory-based development. This style of teaching is conducive to learning how to build real-world products that adhere to industry best practices.

Additionally, Jordan has published multiple books on programming and computer science along with developing training curriculum for Learn.co, DevCamp, and AppDev on the topics, namely Ruby on Rails, Java, AngularJS, NoSQL, API development, and algorithms.

www.PacktPub.com

For support files and downloads related to your book, please visit `www.PacktPub.com`.

Did you know that Packt offers eBook versions of every book published, with PDF and ePub files available? You can upgrade to the eBook version at `www.PacktPub.com`and as a print book customer, you are entitled to a discount on the eBook copy. Get in touch with us at `service@packtpub.com` for more details.

At `www.PacktPub.com`, you can also read a collection of free technical articles, sign up for a range of free newsletters and receive exclusive discounts and offers on Packt books and eBooks.

`https://www.packtpub.com/mapt`

Get the most in-demand software skills with Mapt. Mapt gives you full access to all Packt books and video courses, as well as industry-leading tools to help you plan your personal development and advance your career.

Why subscribe?

- Fully searchable across every book published by Packt
- Copy and paste, print, and bookmark content
- On demand and accessible via a web browser

Customer Feedback

Thanks for purchasing this Packt book. At Packt, quality is at the heart of our editorial process. To help us improve, please leave us an honest review on this book's Amazon page at `https://www.amazon.com/dp/1787280640`.

If you'd like to join our team of regular reviewers, you can e-mail us at `customerreviews@packtpub.com`. We award our regular reviewers with free eBooks and videos in exchange for their valuable feedback. Help us be relentless in improving our products!

Table of Contents

Preface

Coding has become one of the most critical skills you can have for furthering your career. Whether you are an experienced developer who wants to learn a new language or you are new to programming, this course can be your comprehensive Ruby coding guide. Starting with foundational principles, such as syntax and scaling up, to advanced topics, such as metaprogramming and big data analysis, I wanted to create a curriculum that will give you all the tools you need to be a professional Ruby developer. With over a decade of real-world development experience, I have engineered this book to ensure it focuses on the skills you will need to be a professional Ruby developer.

What this book covers

Chapter 1, *Introduction to the Ruby Programming Language*, gives a high-level view of the Ruby programming language, how to install it on your system, and getting it up and running so you can start building Ruby programs.

Chapter 2, *Ruby Variables*, teaches you how to work with variables in Ruby to store data and use the data throughout a program, because Ruby variables are the building blocks of just about every Ruby program.

Chapter 3, *Ruby Strings*, teaches about the Ruby string data type and walks you through how to integrate string data into a Ruby program. Working with words, sentences, and paragraphs are common requirements in many applications.

Chapter 4, *Working with Numbers in Ruby*, explains how to work with different number data types in a Ruby program, including the integer and float types. A key component in building programs is developing mathematical equations in order to implement various algorithms.

Chapter 5, *Ruby Methods*, teaches how to create and use methods in Ruby programs to store processes and reuse them throughout a program, including an overview of procs and lambdas. One of the most powerful tools available to developers is the ability to store functionality and share that behavior throughout a program.

Chapter 6, *Ruby Iterators and Loops*, works you through the powerful iteration tools that come with the Ruby programming language that allow you to traverse various collection types. When it comes to developing programs, one of the common tools utilized by programmers is the ability to loop through collections of data.

Chapter 7, *Ruby Collections,* shows that nearly every application that you will build will need to implement collections of data in some form or another. This could be anything from a database query that returns multiple records to a set of dates in a calendar.

Chapter 8, *Ruby Conditionals,* teaches how to integrate conditionals into a Ruby program, which will enable your programs to have dynamic behavior based on different input data. A key component for building dynamic behavior into Ruby applications requires conditional logic at some stage or another.

Chapter 9, *Object-Oriented Programming in Ruby,* teaches you Object-Oriented Programming (OOP) for Ruby, including creating classes, instantiating objects, working with inheritance, and polymorphism. In addition to readability, one of the defining attributes of the Ruby programming language is how it implements OOP techniques.

Chapter 10, *Working with the Filesystem in Ruby,* reveals various ways to work with files in Ruby, including the ability to create, open, edit, and delete files using built-in methods and classes.

Chapter 11, *Error Handling in Ruby,* explains how to work with errors in Ruby, including how to build practical tools such as an error logging program. Many new developers are intimidated when they come across errors and exceptions in a program. However, errors are Ruby's way of telling you how you can improve or alter your program to work properly.

Chapter 12, *Regular Expressions in Ruby,* enables you to work with regular expressions in Ruby, including the built in Regex class that allows you to build matchers and dynamically search through data. Pattern matching is a common requirement for building code libraries such as validations and basic search functionality.

Chapter 13, *Searching with grep in Ruby,* teaches how to use the powerful grep method in Ruby programs in order to search through data. Ruby offers a wide variety of options when it comes to searching through strings.

Chapter 14, *Ruby Gems,* walks you through and teaches what Ruby gems are, how to use them, and where you can find new gems to give your Ruby programs additional functionality. One of the reasons for Ruby's growth in popularity over the past decade is the open source community building code libraries that can be implemented in other applications. Typically, these code libraries are called Ruby gems.

Chapter 15, *Ruby Metaprogramming*, explains some of the basics of metaprogramming in Ruby, including how to open classes and add functionality to built-in Ruby classes. Writing code that writes code is one of the more challenging topics in any programming language. However, metaprogramming in Ruby offers such a powerful interface for building advanced features into an application. It is worth the effort to learn it.

Chapter 16, *Ruby Web Frameworks*, reveals the two most popular web frameworks for Ruby programs, Rails and Sinatra, including building applications for both frameworks.

Chapter 17, *Working with APIs in Ruby*, walks you through how to work with APIs and build a Ruby program that communicates with a third-party API and parses the JSON data. Working with outside services is a powerful mechanism for building data-driven applications.

Chapter 18, *Ruby Algorithms*, puts together all of the knowledge that we've compiled in the book in order to implement popular algorithms. Specifically, you'll learn how to build advanced algorithms in the Ruby programming language, including the sorting methods, such as quick sort and merge sort, along with a number of functional programming algorithms.

Chapter 19, *Machine Learning*, teaches how to integrate machine learning algorithms into a Ruby program, including how to build a decision tree, train it, and have it output dynamic results. One of the fastest growing sectors in development is machine learning.

What you need for this book

This course starts at the beginning with how to install Ruby and work with it on multiple machines, so simply have a computer that's connected to the internet and you'll be ready. I'll also show how to run Ruby programs in the browser, so you can work through this book on any operating system.

Who this book is for

This is a complete course written from the ground up for beginners wanting to gain a solid understanding of the Ruby language. It starts at the beginning with how to install Ruby and work with it on multiple machines, so simply have a computer that's connected to the Internet and you'll be ready.

Conventions

In this book, you will find a number of text styles that distinguish between different kinds of information. Here are some examples of these styles and an explanation of their meaning.

Code words in text, database table names, folder names, filenames, file extensions, pathnames, dummy URLs, user input, and Twitter handles are shown as follows: "Now if I always want a string to be in lower case letters, I can use the `downcase` method, like this."

A block of code is set as follows:

```
10.times do
  x=10
end

p x
```

When we wish to draw your attention to a particular part of a code block, the relevant lines or items are set in bold:

```
10.times do
  x=10
end

p x
```

Any command-line input or output is written as follows:

```
rvm install 2.3.0
```

New terms and **important words** are shown in bold. Words that you see on the screen, for example, in menus or dialog boxes, appear in the text like this: "When you click on the **Download Ruby** button, it will take you to the following page."

Warnings or important notes appear in a box like this.

Tips and tricks appear like this.

Reader feedback

Feedback from our readers is always welcome. Let us know what you think about this book-what you liked or disliked. Reader feedback is important for us as it helps us develop titles that you will really get the most out of.

To send us general feedback, simply email `feedback@packtpub.com`, and mention the book's title in the subject of your message.

If there is a topic that you have expertise in and you are interested in either writing or contributing to a book, see our author guide at `www.packtpub.com/authors`.

Customer support

Now that you are the proud owner of a Packt book, we have a number of things to help you to get the most from your purchase.

Downloading the example code

You can download the example code files for this book from your account at `http://www.packtpub.com`. If you purchased this book elsewhere, you can visit `http://www.packtpub.com/support` and register to have the files e-mailed directly to you.

You can download the code files by following these steps:

1. Log in or register to our website using your email address and password.
2. Hover the mouse pointer on the **SUPPORT** tab at the top.
3. Click on **Code Downloads & Errata**.
4. Enter the name of the book in the **Search** box.
5. Select the book for which you're looking to download the code files.
6. Choose from the drop-down menu where you purchased this book from.
7. Click on **Code Download**.

Once the file is downloaded, please make sure that you unzip or extract the folder using the latest version of:

- WinRAR / 7-Zip for Windows
- Zipeg / iZip / UnRarX for Mac
- 7-Zip / PeaZip for Linux

The code bundle for the book is also hosted on GitHub at `https://github.com/PacktPubl ishing/Comprehensive-Ruby-Programming`. We also have other code bundles from our rich catalog of books and videos available at `https://github.com/PacktPublishing/`. Check them out!

Downloading the color images of this book

We also provide you with a PDF file that has color images of the screenshots/diagrams used in this book. The color images will help you better understand the changes in the output. You can download this file from `https://www.packtpub.com/sites/default/files/down loads/ComprehensiveRubyProgramming_ColorImages.pdf`.

Errata

Although we have taken every care to ensure the accuracy of our content, mistakes do happen. If you find a mistake in one of our books-maybe a mistake in the text or the code-we would be grateful if you could report this to us. By doing so, you can save other readers from frustration and help us improve subsequent versions of this book. If you find any errata, please report them by visiting `http://www.packtpub.com/submit-errata`, selecting your book, clicking on the **Errata Submission Form** link, and entering the details of your errata. Once your errata are verified, your submission will be accepted and the errata will be uploaded to our website or added to any list of existing errata under the Errata section of that title.

To view the previously submitted errata, go to `https://www.packtpub.com/books/conten t/support`and enter the name of the book in the search field. The required information will appear under the **Errata** section.

Piracy

Piracy of copyrighted material on the Internet is an ongoing problem across all media. At Packt, we take the protection of our copyright and licenses very seriously. If you come across any illegal copies of our works in any form on the Internet, please provide us with the location address or website name immediately so that we can pursue a remedy.

Please contact us at `copyright@packtpub.com` with a link to the suspected pirated material.

We appreciate your help in protecting our authors and our ability to bring you valuable content.

Questions

If you have a problem with any aspect of this book, you can contact us at
questions@packtpub.com, and we will do our best to address the problem.

1
Introduction to the Ruby Programming Language

Welcome to the *Comprehensive Ruby Programming* book! I'm excited to go through all the materials and walk you through this great programming language.

I've been a programmer for more than a decade, and I started Ruby about five years ago. Since then, I absolutely fell in love with Ruby for a wide array of reasons. As you learn the language you'll discover that you spend less time worrying about the syntax and more time coding, which adds to the fun. By the time you're finished with this course I hope you'll love this language as much as I do!

In this chapter, we'll take a high level view of the Ruby programming language, learn how to install it on your system, and get it up and running so you can start building Ruby programs. By the end of this chapter, you will have learnt the following:

- Describe the high level concepts of the Ruby programming language
- Construct the configuration to run Ruby programs
- Define how to work with multiple Ruby versions

What is Ruby?

Ruby is an open source programming language, which means that it's free to use, and it was developed by a large community of developers.

So what can you do with Ruby? By leveraging the Ruby programming language you can build many different types of applications. If you're interested in building dynamic web applications you will most likely want to learn the Ruby on Rails web framework. Since Rails is built on top of Ruby, it's beneficial to understand how to program in Ruby before you can use Rails properly.

Popular sites that use Ruby

So what sites use Ruby?

- `hulu.com`: A popular destination to watch TV shows and movies online
- `twitch.tv`: A video game-viewing site that was acquired by Amazon
- `lumosity.com`: A popular learning platform
- `weheartit.com`: A great entertainment site
- `bloomberg.com`: An application that processes news and financial data to give financial insights to users
- `github.com`: One of the most well-known Git repositories, GitHub enables developers from all over the world to host their code and collaborate with others

Now that you know the kind of applications that we can build with Ruby, let's get started!

Installing Ruby on a computer

Before we can start programming, you'll need to get Ruby installed on your system. I'm going to walk you through how you can install it on your computer regardless of your operating system, and I'll also give you alternate options if you don't want to install Ruby locally (however I highly recommend installing it).

Ruby language dashboard

Let's start by going to http://ruby-lang.org:

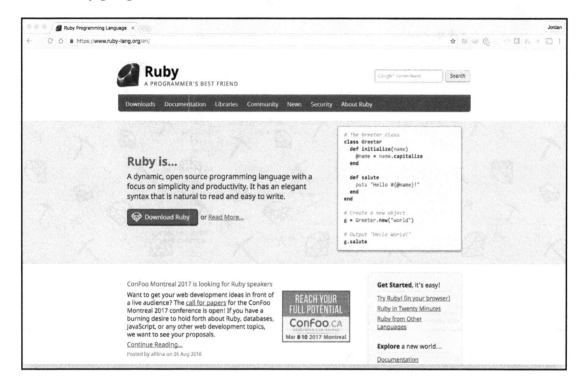

When you click on the **Download Ruby** button, it will take you to the following page:

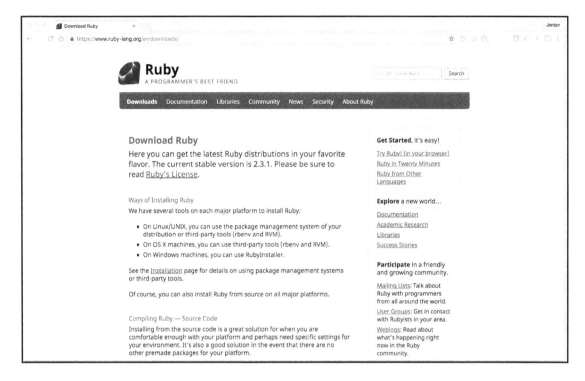

This page gives you information on how to install Ruby on your system.

If you are using the Windows operating system, follow these steps:

1. Go to `rubyinstaller.org`:

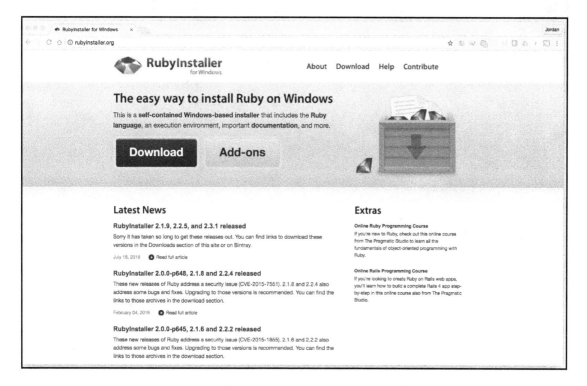

2. From this list, you can pick the stable version you want, I recommend that you go with the latest stable version. When you click on any of these links, the installer will run and you will be ready to go.

If you're using macOS, Ruby is already installed on your system. To check this follow these steps:

1. I created a file called `do_I_have_ruby.rb`, which has only one line of code in it:

   ```
   puts "Yes, you have Ruby!"
   ```

2. Next, go to your Terminal (make sure that you're in the same directory as your Ruby file) and run the file with the following command:

   ```
   ruby do_I_have_ruby.rb
   ```

This should display your string, if Ruby is properly installed:

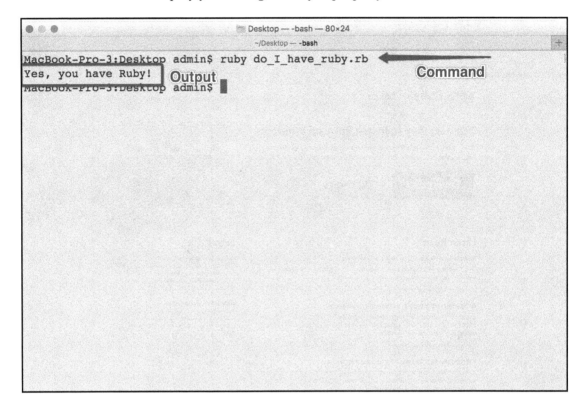

If you don't feel comfortable creating and running a Ruby file like this, you can simply type `irb` into a Terminal window and if it opens up it means that you have Ruby. You can also type `ruby -v` to have the system show you what version of Ruby is installed.

One thing that you can do if you are using the Mac or Linux operating systems is to use the **Ruby Version Manager** (**RVM**). This gives you the flexibility to use different Ruby versions for different projects.

To install RVM, go to `http://rvm.io`, and here you will find the Terminal commands that you can simply copy and paste in your Terminal:

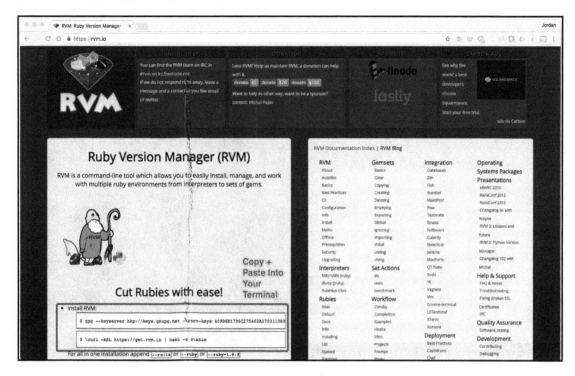

Once you've installed RVM, type `rvm list` and this should list out all the Ruby versions on your system. If you want to change versions you can call the `use` command. For example, type in your Terminal to switch to Ruby version `2.4.0`:

```
rvm 2.4.0
```

If you don't want to install Ruby on your local system, but still want to learn how to build Ruby programs, you can go to `http://repl.it/languages`. This should give you the list of languages available in the `repl.it` dashboard. When you click on Ruby, it will take you to a Terminal that will render all your Ruby code.

I tend to use this site if I have to quickly debug an algorithm or a confusing script. It's a great tool because you're able to get a side-by-side perspective on your code with its output:

So that's how you install Ruby! Now with that installed, you're ready to start learning how to build Ruby programs!

Installing different Ruby versions with RVM

If you're interested in using RVM to manage multiple versions of Ruby on your system, I want to give some more detailed instructions on how you can accomplish this:

1. Start out by going to your Terminal and typing the following command:

    `rvm list`

```
● ● ●                        Desktop — -bash — 80×24
                              ~/Desktop — -bash                              +
[MacBook-Pro-3:Desktop admin$ rvm list

rvm rubies

    ruby-2.0.0-p247 [ x86_64 ]
    ruby-2.0.0-p643 [ x86_64 ]
    ruby-2.1.1 [ x86_64 ]
=*  ruby-2.1.2 [ x86_64 ]
    ruby-2.1.4 [ x86_64 ]
    ruby-2.1.5 [ x86_64 ]
    ruby-2.1.7 [ x86_64 ]
    ruby-2.2.0 [ x86_64 ]
    ruby-2.2.1 [ x86_64 ]
    ruby-2.2.3 [ x86_64 ]
    ruby-2.2.4 [ x86_64 ]
    ruby-2.3.0 [ x86_64 ]

# => - current
# =* - current && default
#  * - default

MacBook-Pro-3:Desktop admin$ ▊
```

If you have RVM installed, this will bring up all of the versions of Ruby that you have access to on your computer.

2. If there is a version of Ruby that you want and that you don't already have on your system, simply type this in to the Terminal:

```
rvm install 2.3.0
```

Running this command will install the 2.3.0 version of Ruby for you:

```
● ◉ ●                    Desktop — -bash — 80×24
                         ~/Desktop — -bash                              +
MacBook-Pro-3:Desktop admin$ rvm list

rvm rubies

   ruby-2.0.0-p247 [ x86_64 ]
   ruby-2.0.0-p643 [ x86_64 ]
   ruby-2.1.1 [ x86_64 ]
=* ruby-2.1.2 [ x86_64 ]
   ruby-2.1.4 [ x86_64 ]
   ruby-2.1.5 [ x86_64 ]
   ruby-2.1.7 [ x86_64 ]
   ruby-2.2.0 [ x86_64 ]
   ruby-2.2.1 [ x86_64 ]
   ruby-2.2.3 [ x86_64 ]
   ruby-2.2.4 [ x86_64 ]
   ruby-2.3.0 [ x86_64 ]

# => - current
# =* - current && default
#  * - default

MacBook-Pro-3:Desktop admin$ rvm use ruby-2.3.0
Using /Users/admin/.rvm/gems/ruby-2.3.0
MacBook-Pro-3:Desktop admin$
```

You can do this for any versions of Ruby that are available via RVM. This makes it easy to ensure you're always using the most up-to-date version of the language. Using RVM is also helpful if you have different projects that utilize various versions of the language. For example, I have some legacy Ruby projects that use Ruby version 1.9.3, while all of my new projects use Ruby 2.3.0 (at the time of writing this guide).

By leveraging RVM, I can quickly switch between different versions of Ruby with a simple Terminal command. Alternatively, if you're not a fan of RVM, you can also use rbenv, which is a similar service.

Summary

In this chapter, we discussed what Ruby is and the popular applications that utilize the Ruby programming language. We also looked at the step-by-step approach of installing Ruby on your computer. With Ruby installed, we also acquired the tools needed to run Ruby programs and go through this book. We later extended our system's functionality and walked through how to install multiple versions of Ruby on our computers, which can be a helpful tool when working with multiple applications that require varying versions of the language.

In the next chapter, we will dive into how to work with variables in Ruby, which will give us the ability to store data and work with it in Ruby programs.

2

Ruby Variables

Ruby variables are the building blocks of just about every Ruby program. In this chapter, you will learn how to work with variables in Ruby to store data and use the data throughout a program. This is a pretty easy chapter and if you're already familiar with Ruby development you can skip this one. After completing this chapter you will be able to do the following:

- Use variables to store data
- Demonstrate how to change variable values

Using variables in Ruby

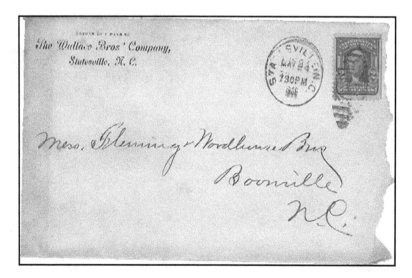

Imagine that you want to send a letter to a friend across the country. Prior to the days of email you would write the letter and place it inside an envelope. Now, the envelope is not the letter itself, instead, envelopes simply hold the letters and allow them to be carried to their destination. In the same way, variables are like envelopes. They store the following:

- Words (also called strings)
- Integers
- Methods
- Collections

The variables themselves are the storage mechanisms for data in Ruby programs. They allow developers to store information in the code and then retrieve the information later on.

Variable code implementation

Now let's dive into the code. For a basic example, I'm going to store my name in a variable:

```
name = "Jordan"
```

If you go to `repl.it` and run this, you can see my name displayed in the Terminal:

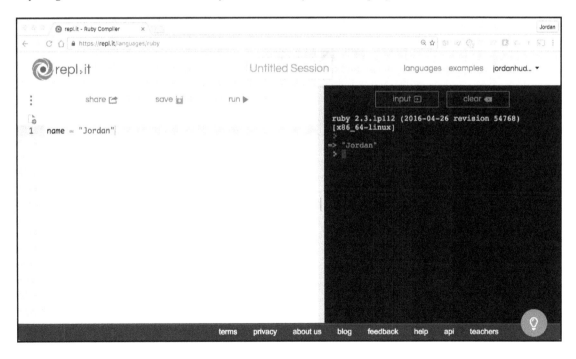

Additionally, a variable can hold more than one value, and in many cases it's called an **array** (for which we will dedicate an entire section, later in this course). Consider this example:

```
address = ["123", "Anystreet", "Anytown", "TX"]
```

Again, in the Terminal, you can see all these values, but they will come with the square brackets. In fact, these brackets denote that it is an array of variables:

Later, we'll walk through how variables can also hold methods, which allow programs to store logic in addition to data that can be called when needed.

As you can see, the syntax for using variables in Ruby is quite straightforward. Unlike many other languages, Ruby variables do not require semicolons or a data type to be declared. This feature is possible because Ruby is a **Just-in-Time** (**JIT**) interpreted language, which automatically recognizes the data type based on what variables are stored.

Printing to the Ruby console

When you're learning a new programming language, it is important to see your program's output. This guide can be used in an online REPL environment (like our variable lesson) or in the Unix Terminal by typing `irb`, which will open an interactive Ruby session.

Using puts

In this lesson, we are going to learn the different options available to print messages to the Ruby console. The first way is to use the `puts` method. Consider this example:

```
puts "A string"
```

The preceding line will display the content, `A string`.

Using p

Another way to print to the console is as follows:

```
p "B string"
```

The difference between these two methods is that the former method will not return any value back to you, whereas the latter one will return a value. The following image shows this difference:

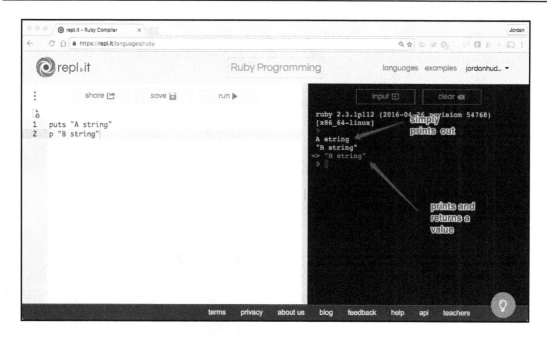

You will see that the `puts` method returns a value of `nil`:

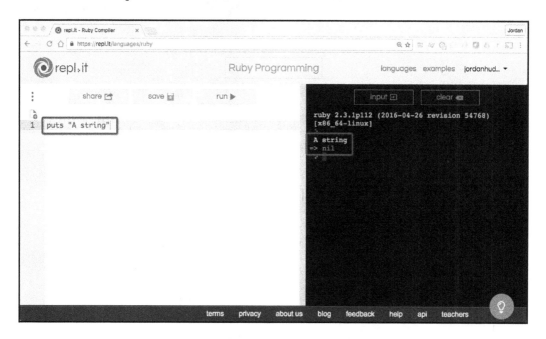

The second option returns the value.

Though this difference may not be much now, you will discover how important this is as we progress through the course.

Another difference between the two methods is the way they process the array data structure. The p method prints the array in its code form and returns these values back to the user:

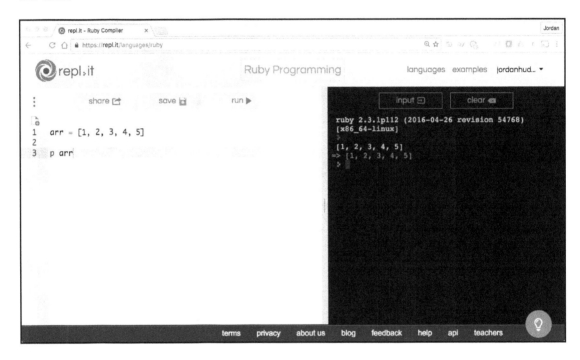

On the other hand, the `puts` method iterates through the collection to display individual values, and as mentioned earlier, this returns a `nil` value:

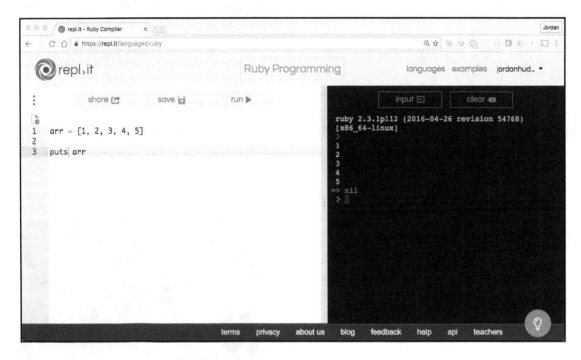

The first set of values were printed with the method.

Knowing that both of these methods work with all data types including arrays and collections is important. Understanding these similarities and differences is important, to ensure that you use the right method at the right time.

Getting input from the Ruby console using gets and chomp

Now that you know how to print values to the console, the next logical step is to know how to get input from users. In this section, we'll walk through how to use the built-in `gets` and `chomp` methods in Ruby.

In a real-world application, you'll most likely use web forms or some tool like that to get an input. However, using console tools you'll be able to mimic what a user types into a program.

Code implementation

We're going to start by asking the question, What is your name? and print that out to the console:

```
puts "What is your name?"
name = gets
```

This code will print the first line to ask the question. In the second line, we are creating a variable called name to hold the value given by the user. The gets method prompts the user to enter a value. So, when you execute this code, this is what you should see:

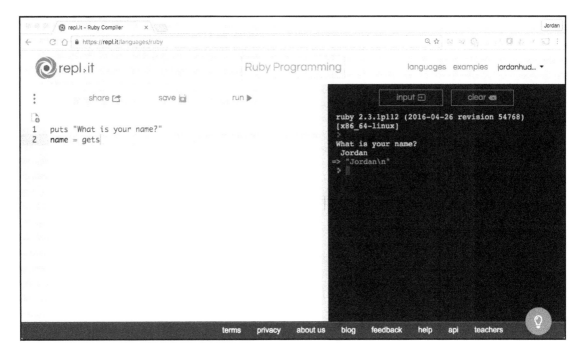

You may notice we have a small problem with `gets`. It returns the value you enter along with the end of line character, `\n`, and this is not something you want to handle in your logic. For example, let's say you want to validate if the user is entering the right password. The code would look like this:

```
puts "Please enter your password:"
password = gets

if password == "asdfasdf"
   true
else
    false
end
```

Now, if you run this code and you enter the password as `asdfasdf`, it will return the value `false` because the value that reaches the application is `asdfasdf\n` and this is not the same as your password:

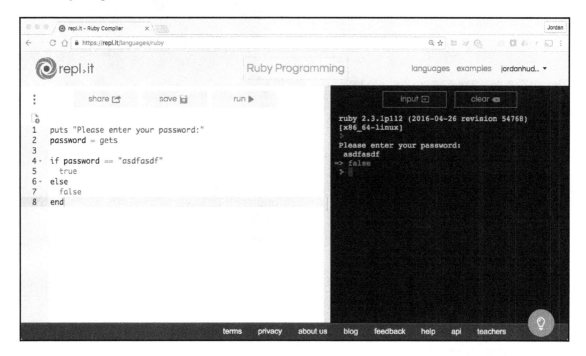

To fix this issue, we can leverage the `chomp` method:

```
password = gets.chomp
```

As the name implies, the word `chomp` gets rid of the `\n` character by chomping it off:

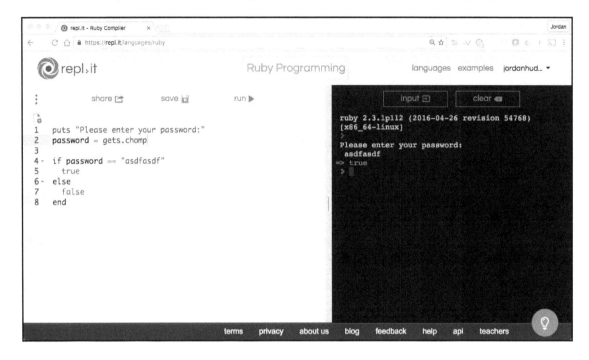

Variable scope and variable types

In this section, we are going to talk about the five different types of variables in Ruby, including how and when they should be used, along with how variable scope works in the Ruby programming language. For this lesson, I will be using the Sublime Text editor instead of `repl.it` so that you can see how Ruby works using files (which is the standard way to build scripts).

The five different Ruby variable types are as follows:

- Local variables
- Global variables
- Instance variables
- Constants
- Class variables

Let's take a look at each of these variable types in detail.

Local variables

Local variables are variables whose scope is limited to the area where they are declared. In other words, if a local variable is declared inside a method or a loop, then its scope is limited to that method or loop.

For example, I am declaring a variable called x and asking it to be printed ten times inside a loop. This is how it will look:

```
10.times do
  x = 10
  p x
end
```

You can now go to the Terminal and run this program. Before that, first check if you're in the right directory by typing the ls command and this will show the files in that directory. In this case, I've named my file as variable_types.rb and I can find this file in the list; and this means I'm in the right place.

Now, to check this code, you need to run the file, and you can do this with the following command:

ruby variable_types.rb

This command will print the value ten times for you.

Now, what happens when you try to print the value of the x variable outside the loop? Logically, you would think x would have the value of 10, and this would be printed only once, since it's outside the loop:

```
10.times do
  x=10
end

p x
```

However, when you run the program, it throws an error:

```
MacBook-Pro:edutechional-ruby admin$ ruby variable_types.rb
variable_types.rb:6:in `<main>': undefined local variable or method `x' for main:Object (NameError)
MacBook-Pro:edutechional-ruby admin$
```

This error occurs because x is a local variable that works only inside the loop and its value is unknown outside the loop. In other words, the system cannot tell you the value of x because it is not available outside the loop.

So, this is the scope of local variables.

Global variables

A global variable is a variable that is available for the entire application to use, and this is denoted by a $ preceding the variable. Now, if you apply the same code, you can see that x is printed. This is how the code should look:

```
10.times do
   $x = 10
end

p $x
```

Now, if you run it in the console, it prints a value of 10.

Though this looks easy, using global variables is not a good idea. In my entire life, I think I've probably used a global variable only once, and now thinking back, I see that there could have been a better way to do it. In general, a global variable is not used because it is hard to track the value of these variables.

Let me give you a scenario. Let's create two files, namely, File1 and File2. In File1, let's assume we have a long algorithm and I create a global variable as a part of this algorithm. For presentation purposes, this is a baseball game and I have my global variable set to Yankees:

```
$global_var = "Yankees"
```

Say another developer who is working on this baseball application with me is working on File2. As a part of his algorithm, he also creates a global variable, but sets it to Astros. So, in File2, we have this code:

```
$global_var = "Astros"
```

So, when someone runs this program, the last file that gets loaded sets the value for this global variable. Also, the developer who created File1 has no idea that the value of global variable was altered to Astros in another file. So, the output will not be what he expects and overall, it can lead to a lot of confusion. This is why it's always a good idea to use variables that have limited scope, such as local or instance variables.

Instance variables

As the name suggests, instance variables are available to a particular instance. There is a specific syntax to set instance variables, you need to use the @ sign to define a variable. For example, keeping in tune with our baseball theme, we can set the batting average like this:

```
@batting_average = 300
```

I'm going to show you how instance variables are used in a real-life Ruby on Rails application:

```
class JobsController < ApplicationController
  before_action :set_job, only: [:show, :edit, :update, :destroy]
  before_action :authenticate_user!, only: [:edit, :new, :destroy]

  # GET /jobs
  # GET /jobs.json
  def index
    @jobs = Job.paginate(page: params[:page], per_page: 10)
  end
```

In the preceding code, you can see that there is an instance variable called @jobs. This variable is created in the index method and is not available to other methods in the file. Now, you may wonder why we wouldn't just make this a local variable since it's not available to other methods in the class.

The reason for this is because Rails is structured in such a way that the view and controller files are wired to communicate with each other, so this instance variable @jobs can be accessed in the associated view file. This is how the view file looks:

```
<% @jobs.each do |job| %>
  <tr style="font-size:1.2em;">
    <td><%= job.created_at.strftime("%m/%d/%y") %></td>
    <td><%= job.req_number %></td>
    <td><%= link_to job.title, job %></td>
    <td><%= job.city %>, <%= job.state %></td>
```

Now, @jobs is available for the view page only because we made it an instance variable in the controller file.

Don't worry if this sounds foreign to you. This is a more advanced development topic and I'm introducing it here so it will look familiar to you when you go through Rails applications. For now, I just want you to understand the scope of an instance variable and how it is different from local variables.

Constants

If you're coming from other programming languages, Ruby handles constants differently than what you may be used to. Constants, in general, take values that do not change through the entire application. The syntax is to use all capital letters while naming your constant so that the application knows how to handle it. For example, to set a constant to hold a baseball team, you would declare it this way:

```
TEAM = "Angels"
```

Typically, other programming languages will not allow you to change the value of `TEAM`. However, Ruby does not hold you back, and it takes the last value assigned to the constant. In the preceding example, I can change its value to:

```
TEAM = "Athletics"
```

Other programming languages would either throw an error or would print the `Angels` value. However, Ruby prints the `Athletics` value because that is the last value assigned to the `TEAM` variable. Also, it gives a warning message which says that the constant was already initialized and was changed because changing a constant is considered a poor programming practice. However, it still lets you make that change and follows the Ruby convention of trusting the developer to make the right programming decision. So, be careful while using constants in Ruby since they can be overridden.

Class variables

Class variables are variables that are available to a particular class. The syntax for this variable is `@@`. Consider this example:

```
class MyClass
  @@teams = ["A's", "Tigers"]
end
```

Though they look simple, you'll rarely use class variables in real-world applications because you can accomplish the same using local or instance variables. Nothing is wrong if you use class variables, but it's not commonly utilized by most developers. In fact, the local and instance variables are likely to make up more than 98 percent of variables in your applications, so it's a good idea to be familiar with them.

Summary

Variables are one of the most fundamental building blocks of programming and after going through this chapter, you should now have a basic understanding of how to use variables in Ruby. We saw two ways to print data out to the Ruby console to see the output. We also looked at how to get user input so that it can be utilized in a program. Additionally, we analyzed how to clean the data by leveraging the chomp method. Lastly, we understood the concept of variable scope and its use.

In the next chapter, we'll dive into the string data type, which is what we use when working with data that contains characters, words, and sentences

3
Ruby Strings

Working with words, sentences, and paragraphs are common requirements in many applications. In this chapter, you'll learn about the Ruby string data type and walk through how to integrate string data into a Ruby program. Additionally, you'll learn how to do the following:

- Employ string manipulation techniques using core Ruby methods
- Demonstrate how to work with the string data type in Ruby

Using strings in Ruby

A string is a data type in Ruby and contains a set of characters, typically normal English text (or whatever natural language you're building your program for), that you would write. A key point for the syntax of strings is that they have to be enclosed in single or double quotes if you want to use them in a program. The program will throw an error if they are not wrapped inside quotation marks.

Let's walk through three scenarios.

Missing quotation marks

In the preceding code, I tried to simply declare a string without wrapping it in quotation marks. As you can see, this results in an error. This error is because Ruby thinks that the values are classes and methods.

Printing strings

In the preceding code snippet, we're printing out a string that we have properly wrapped in quotation marks. Note that both single and double quotation marks work properly.

It's also important that you do not mix the quotation mark types. For example, run the following code:

```
puts "Name an animal'
```

You will get an error, because you need to ensure that every quotation mark is matched with a closing (and matching) quotation mark.

If you start a string with a double quotation mark, the Ruby parser requires that you end the string with a matching double quotation mark.

Storing strings in variables

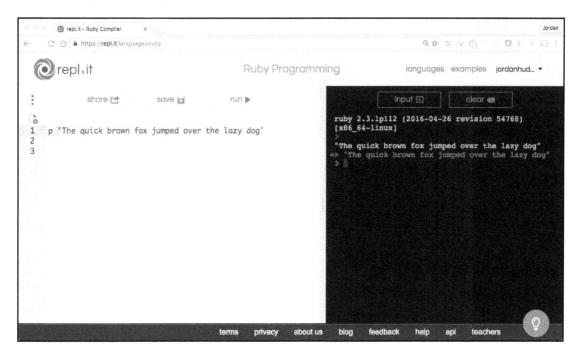

Lastly, in the preceding code snippet, we're storing a string inside of a variable and then printing the value out to the console.

We'll talk more about strings and string interpolation in subsequent sections.

String interpolation guide for Ruby

In this section, we are going to talk about string interpolation in Ruby.

What is string interpolation?

So what exactly is **string interpolation**? Good question. String interpolation is the process of being able to seamlessly integrate dynamic values into a string.

Let's assume we want to slip dynamic words into a string. We can get the input from the console and store that input into variables. From there, we can call the variables inside of a pre-existing string.

For example, let's give a sentence the ability to change based on a user's input:

```
puts "Name an animal"
animal = gets.chomp
puts "Name a noun"
noun= gets.chomp
p "The quick brown #{animal} jumped over the lazy #{noun}"
```

Note the way I insert variables inside the string. They are enclosed in curly brackets and are preceded by a # sign.

If I run this code, this is what my output will look like:

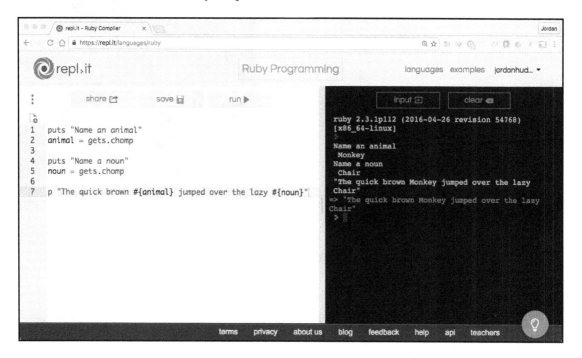

So, this is how you insert values dynamically in your sentences.

If you see sites such as Twitter, it sometimes displays personalized messages such as: **Good morning Jordan** or **Good evening Tiffany**. This type of behavior is made possible by inserting a dynamic value in a fixed part of a string, and it leverages string interpolation.

Now, let's use single quotes instead of double quotes, to see what happens:

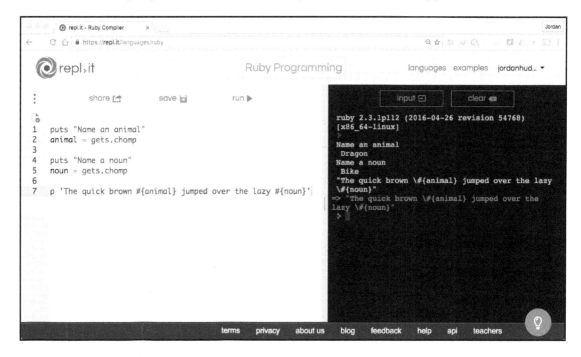

As you'll see, the string was printed as it is, without inserting the values for `animal` and `noun`. This is exactly what happens when you try using single quotes—it prints the entire string as it is without any interpolation. Therefore, it's important to remember the difference.

Another interesting aspect is that anything inside the curly brackets can be a Ruby script. So, technically you can type your entire algorithm inside these curly brackets, and Ruby will run it perfectly for you. However, this is not recommended for practical programming purposes.

For example, I can insert a math equation, and as you'll see it prints the value out:

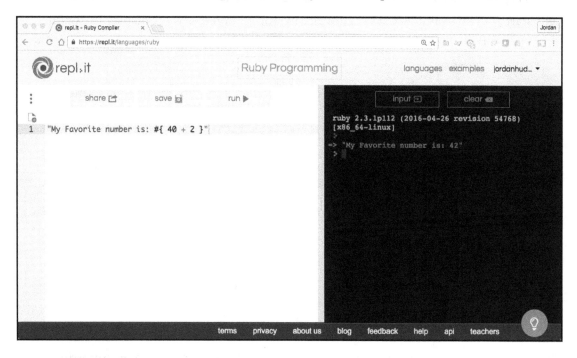

String manipulation guide

In this section, you are going to learn about string manipulation, along with a number of examples of how to integrate string manipulation methods in a Ruby program.

What is string manipulation?

So what exactly is **string manipulation**? It's the process of altering the format or value of a string, usually by leveraging string methods.

String manipulation code examples

Let's start with an example. Let's say I want my application to always display the word `Astros` in capital letters. To do that, I simply write this:

```
"Astros".upcase
```

Now if I always want a string to be in lower case letters, I can use the `downcase` method, like this:

```
"Astros".downcase
```

These are the two methods I use quite often. However, there are other string methods available that we also have at our disposal.

For the rare times when you want to literally swap the case of the letters, you can leverage the `swapcase` method:

```
"Astros".swapcase
```

Lastly, if you want to reverse the order of the letters in the string we can call the `reverse` method:

```
"Astros".reverse
```

These methods are built into the `String` data class and we can call them on any string value in Ruby.

Method chaining

Another neat thing we can do is join different methods together to get a custom output. For example, I can run this:

```
"Astros".reverse.upcase
```

The preceding code displays the `SORTSA` value.

This practice of combining different methods with a dot is called **method chaining**.

A practical implementation

Now, you may be wondering why it's helpful to manipulate strings. It's cool to see, but is there any practical value? Let me walk you through a real-world case study to illustrate the importance of string manipulation.

Whenever I'm building a search engine inside an application that I'm working on, there are many times where I need to convert the case of either the value being searched for or the value from the database. For example, if a user wants to search for the `Milk` word, it's highly likely that my database query will not return the associated record or information because it does not handle case sensitivity well by default. If I have the `milk` word in my database, it wouldn't be returned because database searches are case sensitive. On the other hand, if I convert the entire word to an uppercase or lowercase value, depending on how the database is setup, the database query will work properly and return the correct results. This is one example of the importance of string manipulation in programming.

With regard to string manipulation, we've only touched the basics. Refer to the `String` class documentation (`http://ruby-doc.org/core-2.2.0/String.html`) to see the full list of methods.

Give it a bang!

Before we end this guide, I want to discuss something you may have noticed when it comes to Ruby methods. There are a number of methods that have similar names, with the only difference being that one method will have a ! symbol and the other does not.

 The ! symbol is called bang in Ruby. So if you see a method such as `my_method!`, out loud you'd say *my_method bang*.

Let's take a look at an example of how bang is used for the `upcase` method. The main difference between the two methods is that the bang version will permanently change the value of the variable that the string was stored in.

In general, when the ! symbol is used at the end of a method, it means the original value or string is being changed.

String substitution guide

In this section, we'll walk through a practical string method that enables you to substitute string values that I use in many real-world applications:

```ruby
str = "The quick brown fox jumped over the quick dog"
```

If you notice, I've modified this sentence a bit to have the `quick` word appear twice in my sentence.

Now, if I want to substitute it with the `slow` word, I can use the `sub` method (which is short for substitution):

```ruby
str = "The quick brown fox jumped over the quick dog"
str.sub "quick", "slow"
```

In the preceding code, I'm calling the `sub` method on my `str` string variable and passing two arguments to the `sub` method:

- The first is the word the program has to find
- The second is the replacement word

If I run this code, my output will be `"The slow brown fox jumped over the quick dog"`:

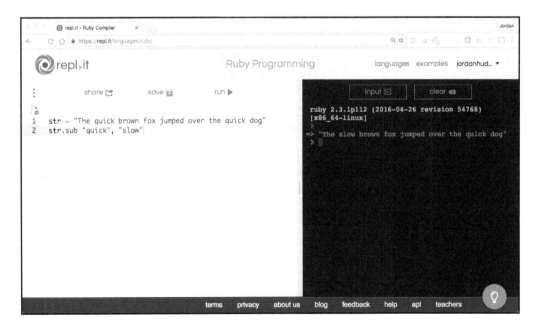

If you notice, this method changes only the first occurrence of the `quick` search word and replaces it with `slow`.

To change all of the occurrences, we need to use the `gsub` method, which stands for global substitution. So, the code should be updated like this:

```
p str.gsub "quick", "slow"
```

If you run this code, the output would be `"The slow brown fox jumped over the slow dog"`:

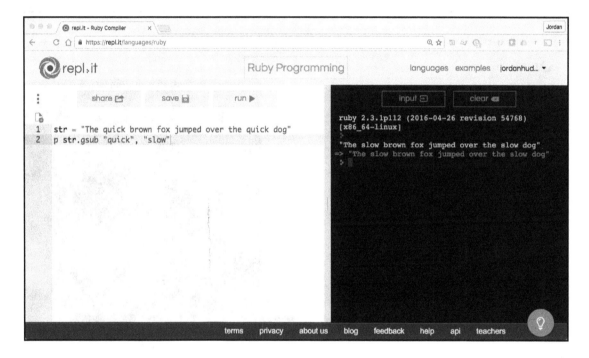

Adding a bang

Now I'm going to show you the difference between `gsub` and `gsub!`.

Going back to the program, if you print the `str` variable out after running through the substitution process, the output will still be "`The quick brown fox jumped over the quick dog`" because the `gsub` method did not change the variable. On the other hand, if you use `gsub!`, and then print the value of `str`, you can see that the `str` variable now has the "`The slow brown fox jumped over the slow dog`" value:

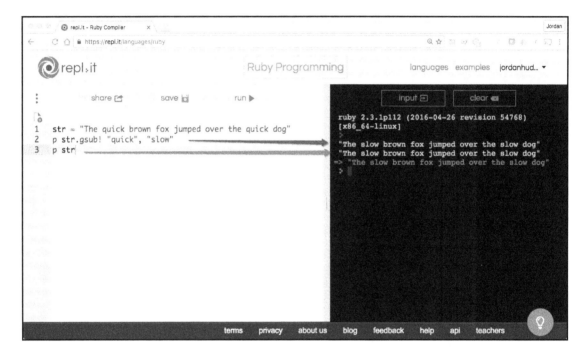

This `gsub!` call can be particularly useful when you want to permanently change the value of the variable. However, you need to be careful, especially when working with legacy systems, because you don't want to accidentally make a permanent change to someone else's variable in case they are expecting a specific value.

Becoming a block head

As great as `gsub` can be by itself, it can become even more powerful when used in conjunction with blocks. Blocks are incredibly useful tools that we'll be using throughout the rest of this book, so we will go into more detail on exactly what blocks are later on. For now, just think of blocks as being tools that allow you to extend the functionality of a method. Let's take a look at another example of how to use `gsub`, but this time we're going to pass in a block:

```
content = "# My Great Headline"
content.gsub(/^.*#.*/) { |heading| "<h1>#{heading[2..-1]}</h1>" }
```

Woah, I know that this code may look weird, don't let it scare you away; let's analyze every process that is going on, along with what the code does. This is the code that parses the markdown language. **Markdown** is a helpful language that allows users to add styles to text files with some basic symbols. For example, passing in the # character tells markdown that the text following the hash symbol should be a headline. So our code looks for the hashtag symbol and wraps the entire line of code with the `<h1>` tags so it can be rendered in a web browser. Now that you know what markdown is, let's analyze the code, bit by bit.

The `/^.*#.*/` code is the argument passed to the `gsub` method. This weird set of characters are called **regular expressions**. We have dedicated an entire chapter to regular expressions later on in the book. For now, just know that regular expressions are coding tools that allow you to match string-based patterns. In the case of our example, we're matching all lines that start with the # character.

So what happens next? Now that the regular expression matches the line of text, the `gsub` method moves down to the curly brackets. In Ruby, a block can be defined by curly brackets (as in the preceding example) or with the `do` and `end` keywords. Inside of the curly brackets we first define a block variable inside of the pipes. This block variable can be called pretty much anything; for our example, I used the `heading` variable name. The block variable is going to represent every match that the `gsub` method brings us. If we were working with a file worth of text, the block variable would represent each time the regular expression was matched. For our basic example, this will be the full content variable. From there, we use string interpolation to wrap the entire match in the `<h1></h1>` tags. And our job is done. The end result will be the `<h1>My Great Headline</h1>` output.

Split, strip, and join guides for strings

In this section, we are going to walk through how to use the `split`, `strip`, `join` methods in Ruby. These methods will help us clean up strings and convert a string to an array so we can access each word as its own value.

Using the strip method

Let's start off by analyzing the `strip` method. Imagine that the input you get from the user or from the database is poorly formatted and contains white spaces before and after the value. To clean the data up, we can use the `strip` method. Consider this example:

```
str = "  The quick brown fox jumped over the quick dog  "
p str.strip
```

When you run this code, the output is just the sentence without the white spaces before and after the words:

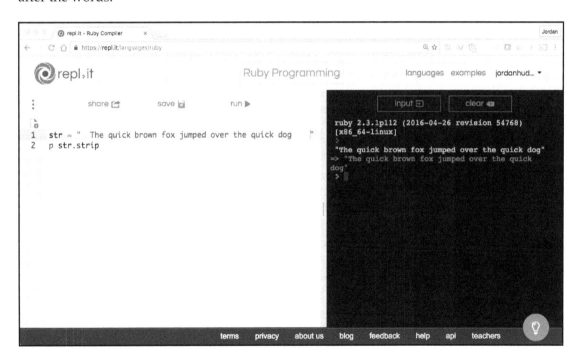

Using the split method

Now let's walk through the `split` method. The `split` method is a powerful tool that allows you to split a sentence into an array of words or characters. For example, type the following code:

```
str = "The quick brown fox jumped over the quick dog"
p str.split
```

You'll see that it converts the sentence into an array of words:

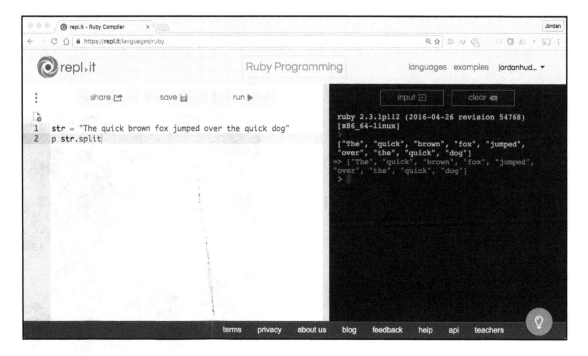

This method can be particularly useful for long paragraphs, especially when you want to know the number of words in the paragraph. Since the `split` method converts the string into an array, you can use all the array methods, like `size`, to see how many words are in the string.

We can leverage method chaining to find out how many words are in the string, as shown here:

```
str = "The quick brown fox jumped over the quick dog"
p str.split.size
```

This should return a value of 9, which is the number of words in the sentence:

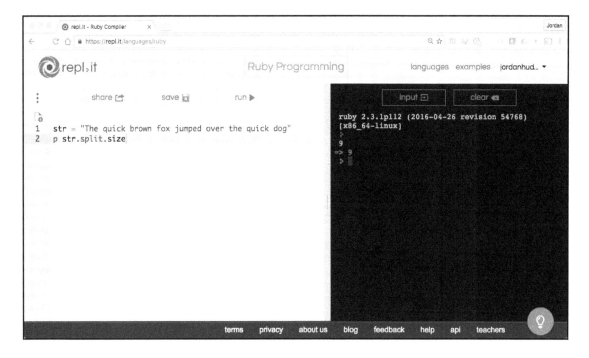

To know the number of letters, we can pass an optional argument to the `split` method and use the following format:

```
str = "The quick brown fox jumped over the quick dog"
p str.split(//).size
```

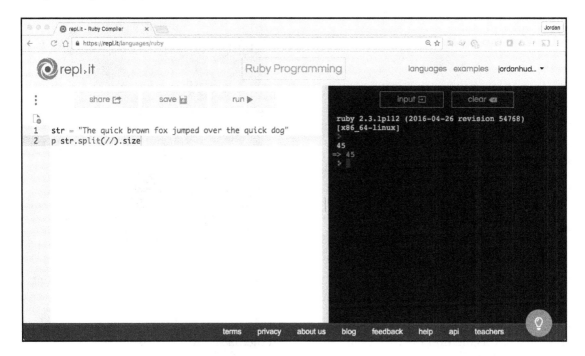

If you want to see all of the individual letters, we can remove the `size` method call, like this:

```
p str.split(//)
```

Your output will now look like this:

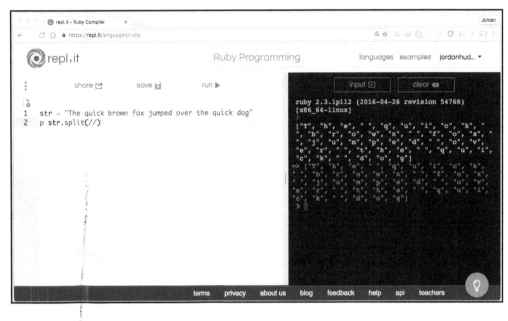

Notice that it also includes spaces as individual characters, which may or may not be what you want a program to return.

This method can be quite handy while developing real-world applications. A good practical example of this method is Twitter. Since this social media site restricts users to 140 characters, this method is sure to be a part of the validation code that counts the number of characters in a Tweet.

Using the join method

We've walked through the `split` method, which allows you to convert a string into a collection of characters. Thankfully, Ruby also has a method that does the opposite, which is to allow you to convert an array of characters into a single string, and that method is called `join`. Let's imagine a situation where we're asked to reverse the words in a string. This is a common Ruby coding interview question, so it's an important concept to understand, since it tests your knowledge of how string works in Ruby. Let's imagine that we have a string, such as this:

```
str = "backwards am I"
```

If we're asked to reverse the words in the string, the pseudocode for the algorithm would be as follows:

1. Split the string into words.
2. Reverse the order of the words.
3. Merge all of the split words back into a single string.

We can actually accomplish each of these requirements in a single line of Ruby code. The following code snippet will perform the task:

```
str.split.reverse.join(' ')
```

This code will convert the single string into an array of strings, for the example, it will equal `["backwards", "am", "I"]`. From there, it will reverse the order of the array elements, so the array will equal `["I", "am", "backwards"]`. With the words reversed, now we simply need to merge the words into a single string, which is where the `join` method comes in. Running the `join` method will convert all of the words in the array into one string.

Summary

In this chapter, you were introduced to the string data type and how it can be utilized in Ruby. We analyzed how to pass strings into Ruby processes by leveraging string interpolation. You also learned the methods of basic string manipulation and how to find and replace string data. We analyzed how to break strings into smaller components along with how to clean up string-based data. We even introduced the `Array` class in this chapter. Don't worry, we're going to dedicate an entire section to collections later in the book, to understand arrays better.

In the next chapter, we're going to transition away from strings and we'll walk through how Ruby works with numbers.

4
Working with Numbers in Ruby

A key component in building programs is developing mathematical equations in order to implement various algorithms. In this chapter, you'll learn how to work with different number data types in a Ruby program, including the integer and float types. Additionally, you will do the following:

- Demonstrate how to work with the integer and float data types in Ruby
- Compute calculations in Ruby with the various number data types

Integer arithmetic guide

Being able to compute mathematical equations in a program is a critical task for most programs in some form or another. In this section, we are going to see how to use integer arithmetic in Ruby.

Performing addition is as simple as a script like this:

```
p 5+5
```

The same applies to subtraction, multiplication, and division. If you want to use exponents, you can use two asterisk symbols, like the following example, where the first 5 is the base integer and the second 5 is the exponent.

```
p 5**5
```

The following is the list of arithmetic functions to use in a Ruby program:

- +: This is used for addition
- −: This is used for subtraction
- /: This is used for division
- *: This is used for multiplication
- **: This is used for exponents

Arithmetic order of operations

When using arithmetic operators, it's important to understand the order of operations, as the compiler uses a specific format to determine this order.

So, what does this order mean for a problem/equation?

Let's say that we need to run an equation with all these operators, but in a different order. For example: 5 + 15 * 20 − 2 / 6 ** 3 − (3 + 1).

In the preceding problem, we have all the six operations included. If we run this code, it gives a value of 301.

To break it down, the compiler first looked for the parentheses, so it computed the value (3+1), which is 4. Then, it handled the exponent 6**3, which is 216. Next is multiplication, so 15 * 20 is 300. Now, for division, 2/216 will be equal to 0 (it's not really zero, but we'll discuss this in the next section). Next, it focuses on addition, 5 + 300 which equals 305. And lastly subtraction: 305 − 4 which equals 301.

You can see the step-by-step path here:

```
5 + 15 * 20 − 2 / 6 ** 3 − (3 + 1)   # parenthesis
5 + 15 * 20 − 2 / 6**3 − 4            # exponents
5 + 15 * 20 − 2 / 216 − 4            # multiplication
5 + 300 − 2 / 216 − 4                # division
5 + 300 − 0 − 4                      # addition
305 − 0 − 4                          # subtraction
301
```

A good way to remember this order is with the acronym **PEMDAS** or with the sentence **Please Excuse My Dear Aunt Sally**.

## Chapter 4

What this stands for is as follows:

- **P**: Parentheses
- **E**: Exponent
- **M**: Multiplication
- **D**: Division
- **A**: Addition
- **S**: Subtraction

Now, this format is not just for numbers but also for other programming components such as conditionals (which we will cover in a future section). Consider this example, where you have a conditional like the following:

```
if (x > 7 && y < 19) || z == 5
```

The value inside the parentheses will get executed first.

Difference between integers and floats

Ruby has a few different data types for working with numbers. Two of the primary options are integer and float. In this section, we're going to walk through the difference between the two data types and how they can affect your program. In the previous section, *Arithmetic order of operations*, you saw a little bit of strange behavior when it came to division. I'm going to bring up the same example. In the code, the division equation, 2 / 216 was treated as 0. We know this is obviously not true, so why did Ruby return this value?

When it saw the values 2 and 216, it treated them as integers. So, it assumed that the user would want a rounded value, so it rounded it to the nearest whole number, which is 0 in this case.

To get the correct answer, we'll need to convert it into a decimal, which will automatically give us a float data type. So, if you run 2.0 / 216, you will get the answer as 0.009259259259259259259259259259926.

This is the difference between the integer and float data types in Ruby. In a real-world application, you are more likely to use the float data type in your database as opposed to integers because you can get more accurate values. In fact, I rarely use integer data type in a real-world application because I want precise values to work with when I'm working with calculations.

Integers are okay to use for items such as an ID; however, make sure to only use them when you know you're not going to be performing calculations with the value.

In general, there are three main number-based data types in Ruby:

- Integer (for example, 1, 2, and 3)
- Float (for example, 1.2, 3.1, and 4.23)
- Decimal (for example, 3.56456456456 and 3.456588990)

The main difference between float and decimal is that the latter gives a more accurate value, even though it is likely to take up more space in your database. This is why decimal is ideal for complex financial applications.

I hope this gives you a clear understanding of the different numerical data types in Ruby.

Summary

This chapter covered some of the critical features of the Ruby language. We walked through the arithmetic operators and the order of operations for arithmetic functions in Ruby. These operators will allow you to perform every combination of computational calculation in your program. We also analyzed the difference between integers and decimals (also referred to as floats), which may not seem like a critical topic; however, an entire NASA rocket was lost due to choosing the incorrect numerical data type, resulting in a loss of millions of dollars!

In the next chapter, we're going to start diving into Ruby methods.

5
Ruby Methods

One of the most powerful tools available to developers is the ability to store functionality and share that behavior throughout a program. In this chapter, you'll learn how to create and use methods in Ruby programs to store processes and reuse them throughout a program, including an overview of procs and lambdas. Additionally, we'll walk through how you can do the following:

- Demonstrate how to build methods in Ruby to encapsulate various processes
- Develop proc- and lambda-based programs and show when to use closures instead of traditional methods
- Recommend how to work with the full list of method argument options, including traditional, splat, named, and default arguments

Creating methods in Ruby

Methods are a powerful feature for building Ruby programs. They allow you to encapsulate behavior and call the method later on to build the functionality of programs. This is an important section, as you are going to learn about methods in Ruby.

Before we walk through the syntax guide, I want to show you a real-world Rails application code file called the `jobs_controller.rb`:

```ruby
1  class JobsController < ApplicationController
2    before_action :set_job, only: [:show, :edit, :update, :destro
3    before_action :authenticate_user!, only: [:edit, :new, :destr
4
5    # GET /jobs
6    # GET /jobs.json
7    def index
8      @jobs = Job.paginate(page: params[:page], per_page: 10)
9    end
10
11   # GET /jobs/1
12   # GET /jobs/1.json
13   def show
14     @job_applications = JobApplication.where(job_id: @job.id)
15   end
16
17   # GET /jobs/new
18   def new
19     @job = Job.new
20   end
21
22   # GET /jobs/1/edit
23   def edit
24   end
25
26   # POST /jobs
27   # POST /jobs.json
28   def create
29     @job = Job.new(job_params)
```

Each one of the items, such as `index`, `show`, `edit`, and `create`, are methods. As you may notice, there are many methods in a file, and each of them performs a specific task, behavior, or action. You are going to be using these methods day in and day out as a Ruby developer, so it's important you have a firm grasp on what the concept is.

Methods have a specific syntax. They begin with the `def` word followed by the name of your method. In general, your method name should reflect its functionality or behavior for easy readability. Also, all the words should be in lowercase and snake case (words joined by an underscore). For example, if I want to create a method that lists out baseball teams, then I would name my method something like this:

```ruby
def baseball_team_list
end
```

Also, methods always end with the `end` word. Your logic goes into the area between the name and the `end` parts of the method. Consider this example:

```
def baseball_team_list
  p ["A's", "Angels", "Astros"]
end
```

To access this method, I can simply call the method by its name:

```
baseball_team_list
```

The logic inside the method will get executed:

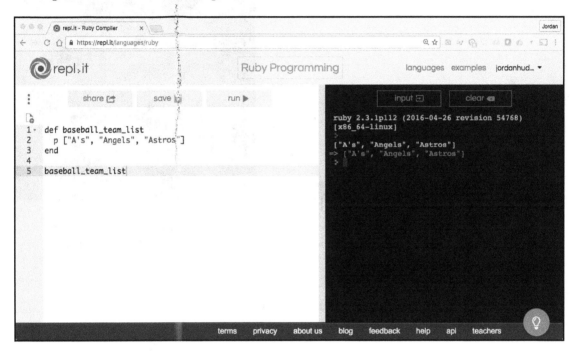

If you run this code without making the call, it will show you that a method called `baseball_team_list` exists with the `baseball_team_list` output:

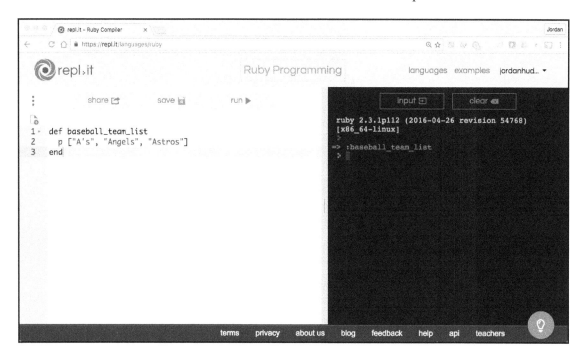

 When you simply run a method, the logic inside it does not get executed. If you want to execute the logic, you have to explicitly call the method.

So, this is how you create and access methods in Ruby.

What does a Ruby method return?

Learning what a method returns is critical in any programming language. Ruby specifically has a unique way of working with returned values. In this section, you are going to learn what a method returns.

I'm going to use the same method we created in the last section, which is as follows:

```
def baseball_team_list
  p ["A's", "Angels", "Astros"]
end

baseball_team_list
```

In other traditional programming languages, you have to explicitly use the `return` word to tell the method to return the values you want. For example, you would have to type something like this:

```
def second_baseball_team_list
  return p ["A's", "Angels", "Astros"]
end

second_baseball_team_list
```

Now, if you hit run, this code will get executed without any errors. However, Ruby does not need an explicit declaration of `return` like this because it is smart enough to know that it has to return the last line of code inside the method. Also, using the `return` word is considered a poor practice for the following reasons:

- We want to avoid using extra code when it's not needed.
- It may confuse experienced Ruby developers. The only time you want to use the `return` word is when you want a method to end prematurely.

You can use the `return` word as a part of a conditional, so that the method returns one set of values when the condition is met, and another set when it is not met. Consider this example:

```
def second_baseball_team_list
  x = 10
  return ["A's", "Angels", "Astros"] if x == 10
  ["yankees", "Mets"]
end

p second_baseball_team_list
```

If you run this method, it returned the `"A's"`, `"Angels"`, `"Astros"` values because the value of x is 10. Also, if you notice, it skipped the second set of teams entirely because when the condition was met, the program simply returns the value and exits. This means that when you have the `return` word, the remaining part of the method does not get executed. Now, if I change the value of x to 15, then it prints `"yankees"` and `"Mets"`.

So, this is the one time you can use the `return` word in Ruby.

What are the differences between class and instance methods in Ruby?

Even though we haven't covered classes in Ruby, I thought it would be good to show you the differences between class and instance methods in Ruby since it's important to see the different behaviors.

For now, you can ignore the class syntax and focus on the functionality, especially the way in which both the method types are called.

I'm going to create a class and add two methods into it, the first being a class method and the second an instance method:

```ruby
class Invoice
  # Class method
  def self.print_out
    "Printed out invoice"
  end

  # Instance method
  def convert_to_pdf
    "Converted to PDF"
  end
end
```

If you notice, the only difference in the syntax is that I used the `self` word for class methods, and the name by itself for instance methods.

Now, when I want to call the class method, I'm able to declare the name of the class followed by a period and then the method name, as shown here:

```
Invoice.print_out
```

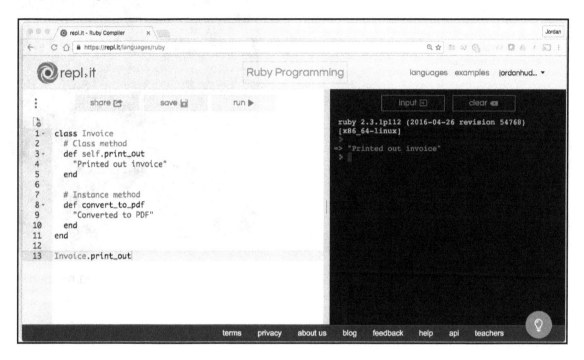

Now, if I try to call the instance method with the same syntax, it throws an error:

You will notice that the error message says that `convert_to_pdf` is an undefined method. In order to run instance methods, we need to create an instance of that class to run it.

I'll give you a hint of what we'll see in the OOP section and we'll instantiate a new `Invoice` like this:

```
i = Invoice.new
i.convert_to_pdf
```

When you run this method, it prints the message without an error:

Now, if I try to access my class method in the same manner that I called the instance method, it will result in an error, as shown here:

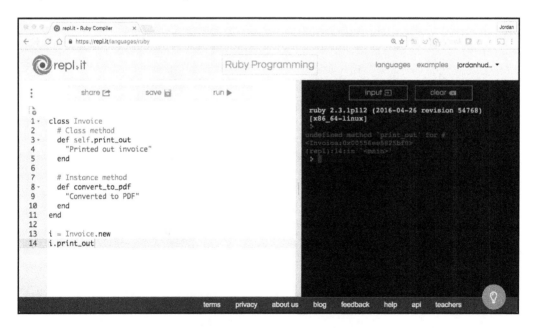

So, a class method can be called in conjunction with the name of the class, whereas the instance method requires you to create an instance to call the method.

As a side note, I can shortcut my code a bit to call my instance method on the same line as the class name:

```
Invoice.new.convert_to_pdf
```

This will work properly. However, typically, it makes no sense to call a method this way because you're not going to be able to do much with it. So, the earlier way of accessing an instance method is better.

You may be wondering why you need an instance method at all when it's so much easier to call a class method.

Let's imagine that you have 15 methods in your class, you wouldn't want to call the class that many times in your program. Consider this example:

```
class Invoice
  # 15 methods inside
end

Invoice.method_1
Invoice.method_2
Invoice.method_3
Invoice.method_4
Invoice.method_5
Invoice.method_6
Invoice.method_7
Invoice.method_8
Invoice.method_9
Invoice.method_10
Invoice.method_11
Invoice.method_12
Invoice.method_13
Invoice.method_14
Invoice.method_15
```

Calling the class every time doesn't look good and is considered to be bad programming practice. Essentially, this is creating 15 new objects in the program.

Creating an instance variable and calling all the methods with it is a better practice:

```
class Invoice
  # 15 methods inside
end
```

```
i = Invoice.new
i.method_1
i.method_2
i.method_3
i.method_4
i.method_5
i.method_6
i.method_7
i.method_8
i.method_9
i.method_10
i.method_11
i.method_12
i.method_13
i.method_14
i.method_15
```

This way you're not creating a new instance of the class every time, instead you're using the same instance for all methods.

I hope this gives you an idea of the different types of methods available in Ruby and how to call them.

Ruby proc tutorial

In this section, we are going to examine the `Proc` module in Ruby. At a high level, procs are methods that can be stored inside variables.

Proc code example

Let's begin by creating a simple proc:

```
full_name = Proc.new{ |first, last| first + " " + last}
```

Now, I can call this in two ways:

- The first is to use the bracket syntax followed by the arguments I want to pass to it:

```
p full_name["Jordan", "Hudgens"]
```

- I can also use the `call` method to run the proc and pass in the arguments inside of parentheses:

```
p full_name.call("Jordan", "Hudgens")
```

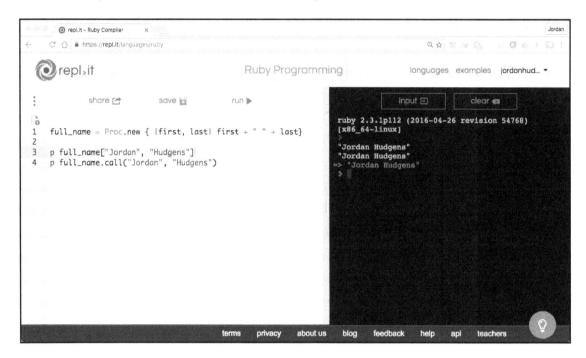

Let's go back and retrace the proc process. In this code, I'm creating a new instance of `Proc` and assigning it to a variable called `full_name`. Procs can take a code block as their parameter, so we are passing two different arguments to them, namely, `first` and `last`. Since they are arguments, they go inside pipes.

I can do anything I want inside this code block; in this case, I'm simply displaying the first and last name. I can also change it to do something like printing my first name five times. To do this, I have to modify the code like this:

```
full_name = Proc.new{ |first| first * 5}
```

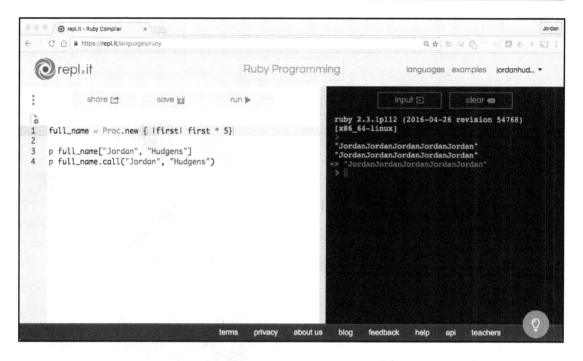

We also have another way to create a proc:

```ruby
full_name = Proc.new  do |first|
    first * 5
end
```

You may notice that I'm only passing in a single argument to the proc and there is no error. This is one of the key differences between using procs versus lambdas, and we'll also dedicate an entire section to the other ways in which they're different, later in this chapter.

The preceding code will result in the same output:

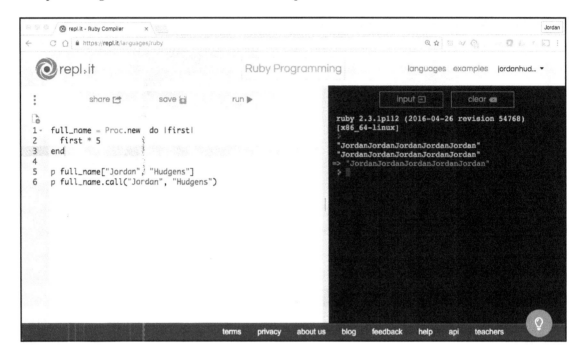

What is a block?

So what exactly is a block? In other programming languages, a block is called a **closure**. **Blocks** allow you to group statements together and encapsulate behavior.

There are two ways to create blocks in Ruby and we'll use a proc to illustrate them:

- Using curly braces

  We'll begin by illustrating how to use blocks with the curly braces syntax, as shown here:

  ```
  add = Proc.new { |x, y| x + y}
  add[1, 2]
  ```

  Running this code will return 3. The code inside of the curly braces is inside the block

- Using `do...end`

The alternate way to use blocks is using the `do...end` syntax:

```
add = Proc.new do |x, y|
  x + y
end

add[1, 2]
```

This will give you the same result as when we used the curly bracket syntax. A rule of thumb in Ruby is to use curly braces when you want to have all logic on the same line. Technically, you can write your program in a single line if you use curly braces.

The next obvious question is: why use procs when you can use methods to perform the same functionality? The answer is that procs give you more flexibility than methods. With procs you can store an entire set of processes inside a variable and then call the variable anywhere else in your program.

The Ruby lambda tutorial

Similar to procs, lambdas allow you to store functions inside a variable and call the method from other parts of a program. In this lesson, we will discuss lambdas and show how to integrate them into a Ruby program.

To get started, I'll use the same example as the previous section, but with a different syntax.

```
full_name = lambda { |first, last| first + " " + last }
```

You can also call lambdas in the same way as procs:

```
p full_name["jordan", "hudgens"]
```

Notice that the implementation is nearly identical to using procs, with the only difference being the use of the `lambda` word instead of `Proc.new`.

Stabby lambdas

In real-world projects, it's a common practice to use a different syntax though—the stabby lambda. Here is how you can use stabby lambdas:

```
full_name = -> (first, last) { first + " " + last }
```

If you run this code, it runs exactly the same way as the previous one.

Like procs, you can also run the lambdas with the `call` syntax:

```
p first_name.call("jordan", "hudgens")
```

So, that's how you create lambdas in Ruby with both the regular and stabby syntaxes.

What is the difference between procs and lambdas in Ruby?

Now that we've seen procs and lambdas, I think it's important to clarify the difference between the two. There are two key differences in addition to the syntax. Note that the differences are subtle, even to the point that you may never even notice them while programming. Still, they're good to know, especially, if you plan on building advanced programs.

Argument count

The first key difference is that lambdas count the arguments you pass to them, whereas procs do not. Consider this example:

```
full_name = lambda { |first, last| first + " " + last}
p full_name.call("Jordan", "Hudgens")
```

Running this code will work properly. However, observe it when I pass another argument like this:

```
p full_name.call("Jordan", "David", "Hudgens")
```

The application throws an error saying that we're passing in the wrong number of arguments:

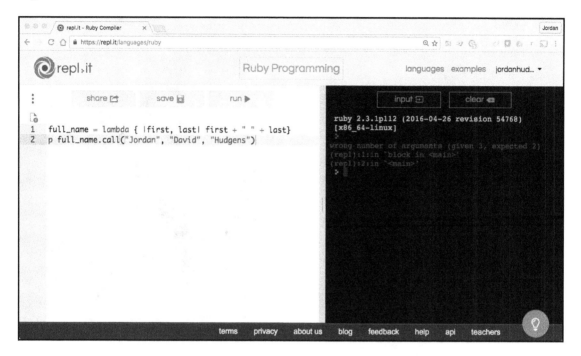

Now, let's see what happens with procs:

```
full_name = Proc.new{ |first, last| first + " " + last}
p full_name.call("Jordan", "David", "Hudgens")
```

If you run this code, you can see that it does not throw an error. It simply looks at the first two arguments and ignores anything after that.

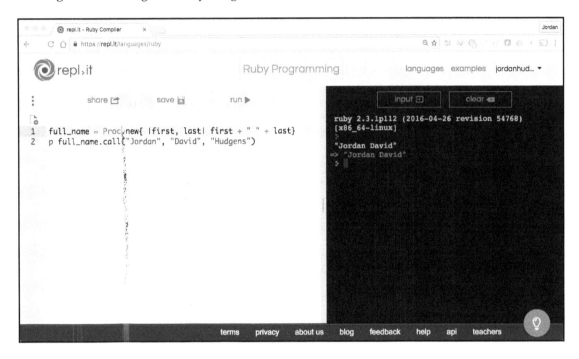

In review, lambdas count the arguments passed to them, whereas procs don't.

Return behavior

Secondly, lambdas and procs have different behaviors when it comes to returning values from methods. To see this, I'm going to create a method called `my_method`:

```ruby
def my_method
  x = lambda  {return}
  x.call
  p "Text within the method"
end

my_method
```

If I run this method, it prints out `"Text within the method"`:

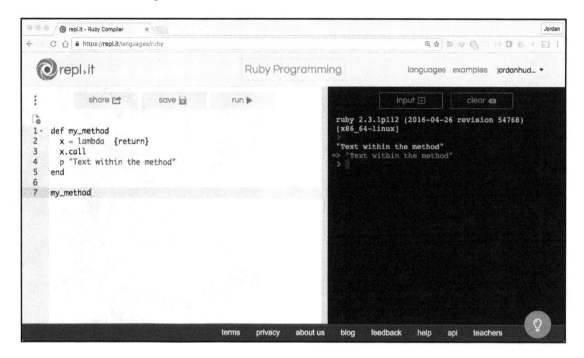

Now, let's try exactly the same implementation with a proc:

```ruby
def my_method
  x = Proc.new {return}
  x.call
  p "Text within the method"
end

my_method
```

When you run it this time, it returns a value of `nil`.

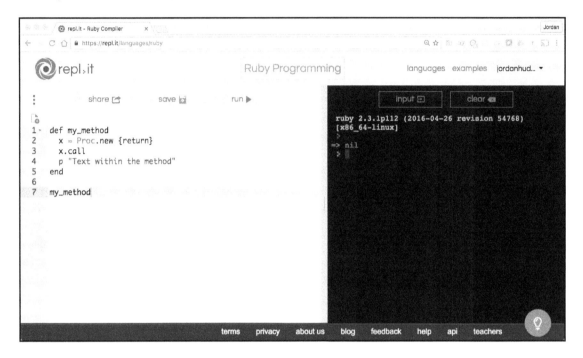

What happened is that when the proc saw the `return` word, it exited out of the entire method and returned a `nil` value. However, in the case of the lambda, it processed the remaining part of the method.

So, these are the subtle and yet important differences between lambdas and procs.

Guide to method arguments in Ruby

In this section, we will examine the various ways to pass arguments to methods in Ruby programs, including the following:

- The argument syntax
- Named arguments
- Default argument values

What are method arguments?

Before we can get into the code examples, let's first walk through what method arguments are. Let's begin with a real-world example:

Imagine that you have a machine that makes baseball bats. The workflow for the bat making process would be as follows:

1. The raw wood is placed in the machine.
2. From there, the machine takes the wood, cuts, and polishes it.
3. Lastly, it finishes off by giving the output as the finished baseball bats from the machine.

So let's see how this analogy applies to the methods in Ruby:

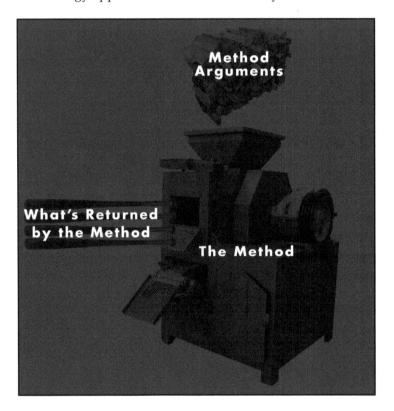

- **Method arguments**: The raw wood placed inside the machine represents the method arguments. This is the data that can be provided by a user, a database query, an API, and so on. It is rare for a method not to have arguments, since method arguments are what allow for dynamic behavior. Looking back at our example, would it be possible to produce the baseball bats if we didn't first supply the machine with the raw materials? Of course not. In the same way, methods need data in order to work with.

- **The method**: The machine itself represents the method. This is where the actual logic goes that will produce the desired behavior.
- **The returned values**: Lastly, the finished bats are like the values that get returned by the methods.

Method argument syntax

Now that you have a good idea on how methods work, let's walk through how we can pass arguments to them.

Method argument code examples

I'm going to start with a very basic example that prints out a user's full name. This is actually a code snippet I took from a real-world code project:

```ruby
def full_name(first_name, last_name)
   first_name + " " + last_name
end

puts full_name("Jordan", "Hudgens")
```

As you'll see, this prints out my full name.

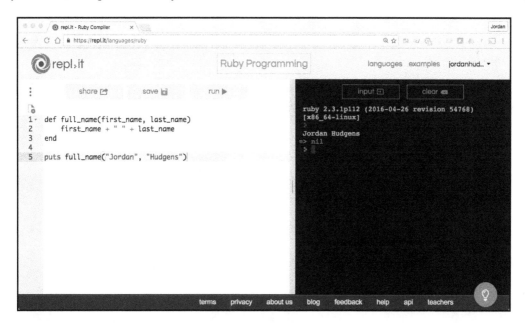

The syntax for how to pass arguments to a method is to simply list them off on the same line that you declare the method. From here, you can treat the names that you supplied as arguments (in this case, `first_name` and `last_name`) as variables in the method.

Now there is also an alternative syntax that we can use that's quite popular among Ruby developers for passing arguments to methods. Here is a slightly updated version of the code example from earlier:

```
def full_name first_name, last_name
  first_name + " " + last_name
end

puts full_name"Jordan", "Hudgens"
```

Notice how all of the parentheses have been taken away? There is some debate on which option is better. I personally prefer to write less code when I have the chance to, so I prefer the second syntax. However both options will work well.

Named arguments

Additionally, Ruby gives us the ability to name our arguments. This can be helpful when you have method signatures with a number of arguments and you want the method calls to be explicit. Here is how you can use named arguments in Ruby:

```
def print_address city:, state:, zip:
  puts city
  puts state
  puts zip
end

print_address city: "Scottsdale", state: "AZ", zip: "85251"
```

If you run this code, it will work properly.

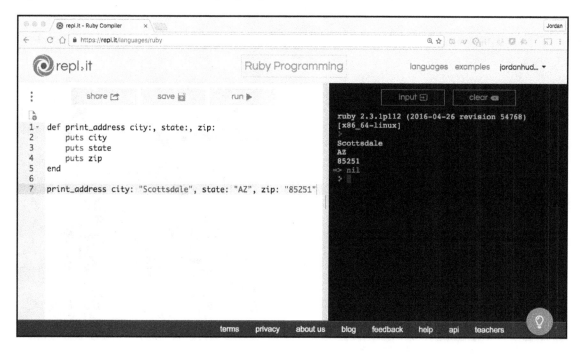

So why are named arguments helpful? I think the easiest way to answer that question is to update our code and remove the named components. That code would look like this:

```
def print_address city, state, zip
    puts city
    puts state
    puts zip
end

print_address "Scottsdale", "AZ", "85251"
```

If you run this code, it will work exactly as it did earlier.

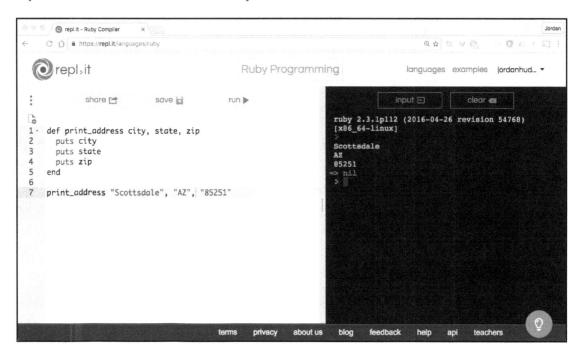

However, by removing the named arguments, we've made our method more difficult to work with and more prone to bugs. When working with a method as simple as `print_address`, it's easy to know what the `city`, `state`, and `zip` parameters represent and to provide them in that order. However, what if we had a method that looked like this:

```
def sms_generatorapi_key, num, msg, locale
  # Magic SMS stuff...
end
```

In a case like this, we would have to reference the method declaration several times to ensure we're passing in the arguments properly. See what would happen if we tried to call this method with the code:

```
sms_generator "82u3ojerw", "hey there", 5555555555, 'US'
```

Nothing looks wrong with this code, right? Actually, this code won't work because we've accidentally swapped the order of the phone number and message. In a real application, the method would try to send the SMS to the `hey there` string, which wouldn't work for obvious reasons.

However, if we update this method to use named arguments, the order no longer matters:

```
def sms_generatorapi_key:, num:, msg:, locale:
  # Magic SMS stuff...
end

sms_generatorapi_key: "82u3ojerw", msg: "hey there", num: 5555555555,
locale: 'US'
```

When you utilize named arguments, you don't have to worry about the order that you pass the arguments in, which is a nice convenience and will also help prevent bugs in your program.

Default argument values

We'll finish up our discussion on Ruby method arguments by discussing default values. There are many times when you'll want to supply default values for an argument and Ruby let's you implement this functionality quite easily.

Let's take the example of building a method that streams movies. We'll need the user to tell the method which movie to watch; however, we don't want them to have to enter in the language for the movie unless it's other than English. In cases like this, we can use the default values with this syntax:

```
def stream_movie title:, lang: lang = 'English'
  puts title
  puts lang
end

stream_movie title: 'The Fountainhead'
```

As you can see, this works properly and prints out `English` as the language because we declared it as a default language.

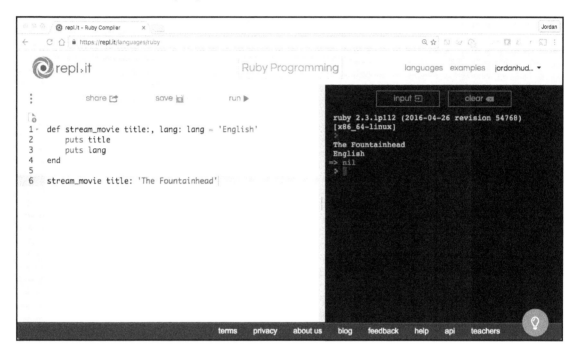

Now if we want to watch a movie in Spanish, we can optionally pass in the `lang` argument into the method call:

```
stream_movie title: 'The Fountainhead', lang: 'Spanish'
```

I hope that this has been a helpful guide to how you can use method arguments in Ruby. In the next section, we'll walk through the splat and optional argument components that Ruby allows.

Using splat and optional arguments in Ruby methods

This section explains how to use the splat and optional argument types with Ruby methods to give flexible interfaces to programs. So far, we've covered traditional, named, and default arguments. However, Ruby isn't done yet. When it comes to passing data to methods, Ruby gives a few more key tools that we can use:

- Traditional splat arguments
- Keyword-based splat arguments
- Optional arguments

Traditional splat arguments

One of my favorite features in Ruby is how explicit many of its methods are, and splat may be one of my preferred arguments. The splat argument allows developers to pass an array of values into a method. Imagine that we are building a program that manages a baseball team. If we had a `roster` method that printed out all of the player names, it would be messy to try to pass all of the names into the method one by one.

For example, this is what it would look like if we simply tried to pass three players into the method manually:

```
def roster player1, player2, player3
  puts player1
  puts player2
  puts player3
end
roster 'Altuve', 'Gattis', 'Springer'
```

Technically, this code would work. However, this is a trivial example; a baseball team keeps 40 players on its roster. I wouldn't even be able to fit the method on a single page if I tried passing in all of the players one by one. Thankfully, this is where Ruby's splat tool comes into play.

We can refactor our code to look like this:

```
def roster *players
  puts players
end

roster 'Altuve', 'Gattis', 'Springer'
```

The syntax for using the splat operator is to put an asterisk in front of the argument name. From that point, you can pass one or any number of values to the method and they'll all be stored in the splat argument.

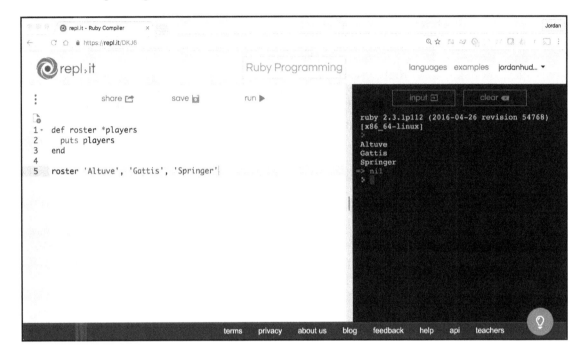

Once inside the method, you can treat the argument like an array (I know we haven't covered arrays yet; however, for now, think about them as a collection of objects).

This is a powerful tool because there are plenty of times when you're going to need to pass values to a method, but you won't always know the exact number of items. In cases like this, splat is very handy.

Keyword-based splat arguments

In addition to regular splat arguments that are essentially flexible containers for arguments, Ruby also allows for keyword-based splat arguments. You can think about this tool as a cross between splat and keyword arguments.

Extending our baseball `roster` method, let's imagine that we need to give it the ability to print out the full list of players and positions. By leveraging keyword-based splat arguments, we can accomplish this feature. The following is the code for this feature:

```ruby
def roster **players_with_positions
  players_with_positions.each do |player, position|
    puts "Player: #{player}"
    puts "Position: #{position}" puts "\n"
  end
end

data = {
  "Altuve": "2nd Base",
  "Alex Bregman": "3rd Base",
  "Evan Gattis": "Catcher",
  "George Springer": "OF"
}

roster data
```

Here we're storing our players and positions in a Ruby hash data structure called `data`. We'll cover hashes later on in the book. For now, just be aware that hashes let you store key/value-based data:

In our `roster` method, we're declaring that we're using the keyword-based splat operator by putting the double asterisk in front of the argument. Inside of the method, we're looping over the data and printing out the respective player and position values. Notice how we can place block arguments inside the pipes (`player` and `position` in this case) that we can call with `each` loop iteration.

This is a great technique to use if you're working with dynamic data that has a specific key/value-based kind of structure. This is common when using database queries.

Optional arguments

Last on our list of method arguments is the ability to pass optional arguments to a method. There are a number of times when you want flexibility with what types of data you pass to methods, and that's where optional arguments can come in handy.

Let's imagine that we're creating an `invoice` method. Our implementation needs to be flexible because some customers provide different data than others. We can accommodate this type of behavior using code like this:

```
def invoice options={}
  puts options[:company]
  puts options[:total]
  puts options[:something_else]
end

invoice company: "Google", total: 123, state: "AZ"
```

When we run this program, you can see some interesting behavior. We're using the `options` hash in our method declaration. The `options` term is not required; you could use any word, but `options` is considered as a standard term to use:

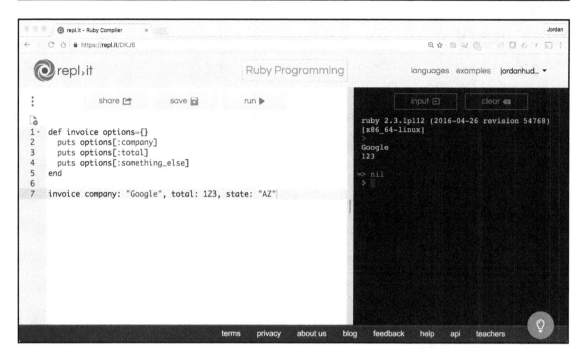

From this point, we can use the syntax such as options[:company] to grab the parameters that we want to use. There is a clear mapping between the name we call inside the method and the named argument we pass when we call the method. Also of note (and warning) is that this type of tool can cause silent bugs in your program. Do you notice how I attempted to print out options[:something_else] and I also passed an additional argument of state: "AZ" into the program? However, these items did not throw an error. This means that you need to be careful when you use optional arguments because they won't fail, they simply won't do anything.

Summary

In this chapter, you were introduced to methods in Ruby and what methods return. We also examined the two types of method available in Ruby programs. The difference between the two method types may seem subtle right now; however, the difference between method types reveals itself when working with Ruby on Rails applications. For now, the key takeaway is that there are two options for method types in Ruby. This chapter also walked you through a close cousin to methods—the proc. We also saw what lambdas are and how to encapsulate entire blocks of behavior with lambdas. Additionally, we walked through how to pass arguments to lambdas in order to have data-driven features. We examined the key differences between procs and lambdas. We also looked at the various ways to pass arguments to methods. We analyzed how to implement splat and optional arguments in methods which allow for flexibility with regard to passing data into methods.

In the next chapter, we're going to dive into loops and enumerable methods.

6
Ruby Iterators and Loops

When it comes to developing programs, one of the common tools utilized by programmers is the ability to loop through collections of data. In this chapter, we will work through the powerful iteration tools that come with the Ruby programming language that allow you to traverse various collection types. Additionally, you will be able to do the following:

- Demonstrate how looping and iteration are able to perform sequential processes
- Use Ruby's `Enumerable` class to perform functional programming processes

The while loop guide

We're going to start this section on loops with one of the most primitive ways of iterating through a collection—the `while` loop.

The `while` loops are rarely used in Ruby development; however, they will offer a solid foundation for the other tools that we can use to work with sets of data. If you're coming from another programming language, you are most likely already familiar with the `while` loops.

The while loop code example

The following is the code for a basic `while` loop:

```
i = 0

while i < 10
  puts "Hey there"
  i += 1
end
```

Let's walk through the steps for building a `while` loop in Ruby:

1. We have to create a variable that will work as a counter and set it equal to `0`.
2. Then we declare the conditional which you can read as: while `i` is less than `10`, continue looping.
3. Inside the loop, we place the code we want to be executed each time the loop runs.
4. We increment our `i` loop variable by `1` with each iteration. This is required to prevent an infinite loop from occurring. An **infinite loop** is what happens when you forget to tell the loop when it can stop and it will eventually crash the program.
5. Lastly, we supply the `end` keyword to designate where the loop code ends.

If you run this code, you can see the following output:

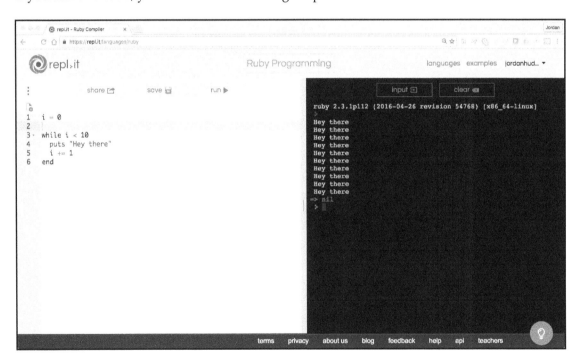

If you count, you can see it printed the `Hey there` string ten times.

This output may sometimes be confusing because we asked the code to print a message when `i` was less than `10`, so why did it print it ten times?

Before I explain this behavior, let's update the code slight by using the <= operator (which stands for less than or equal to):

```
i = 0

while i<= 10
    puts "Hey there"
    i += 1
end
```

When you run this code, you can see the following output:

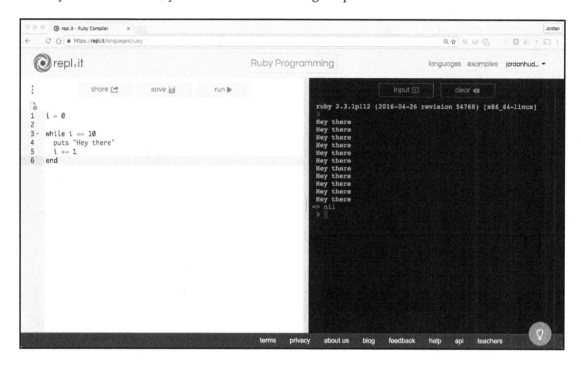

If you notice, the message was printed 11 times.

This is because the value of i started at 0. So, it ran the first time and was incremented after iterating through the loop. Whenever using a `while` loop, it's important to understand what criteria will cause it to end or you may end up with slightly different results than what you wanted.

One thing to keep in mind when using `while` loops is to always increment the value of the loop variable. Because if you don't, the value of i will always be 0, and the loop will simply continue to run until the program crashes.

Also, if you notice, Ruby does not have an increment operator such as ++, which can be found in other languages. So when you want to increment a value by one in Ruby you need to do it manually, like this:

```
i = i + 1
```

You can alternatively use the shortcut syntax that I used in the `while` loop:

```
i += 1
```

 There is nothing special with using the `i` variable name. You could use any variable name that you want as long as the name matches the other parts of the program.

The each iterator method tutorial

Being able to cycle through a list of values is something that you'll be doing on a daily basis when working with Ruby programs. In this section, we are going to go through Ruby's popular iterator—the `each` loop.

You already learned how to use `while` loops. If you remember, there were a number of different rules for ensuring that our `while` loops were processed a specific number of times. We also had to ensure that we didn't run into an infinite loop that would crash our program. It's for these reasons that `while` loops aren't utilized in Ruby very often. Instead, the `each` mechanism is the tool of choice when it comes to looping over collections.

The each loop code example

Before we can use the `each` loop, we need to create a collection that it can work with. For simplicity's sake, and since we haven't gotten to our array, I'm going to use a very basic array of integers:

```
arr = [23, 2343, 454, 123, 345345, 1232]
```

Now that we have a collection to work with, we can implement an `each` loop:

```
arr.each do |i|
  p i
end
```

If you run this, you can see the values in the array printed out. Also notice that the `each` tool gives us the ability to use a block variable. In this case, the block variable is `i` and we place it in between the pipes. This block variable will give us access to each value in the array as the loop iterates through the collection. For our example, with the first iteration, `i` will be set to `23`, the second time through, it will be set to `2343`, and so on. This is a helpful tool because it allows us to work with each element in the collection. For example, if it was an array of strings that we wanted to capitalize, we could loop through and have the `i.upcase` code inside the block and all of the strings would be printed out as uppercase values:

In referencing what you learned about blocks, you have already guessed that we can also swap out our `do...end` block for curly braces. So the same code could be written out this way as well:

```
arr.each{ |i| p i }
```

If you run this code, you'll get the same result. However, make sure you follow the Ruby block rule of thumb, where you only place the code on the same line if it's small and concise.

Now, I want to show you a real-world example of how to use the `each` loop. This code is taken from a Ruby on Rails project that I built:

```
44    <% @jobs.each do |job| %>
45      <tr style="font-size:1.2em;">
46        <td><%= job.created_at.strftime("%m/%d/%y") %></td>
47        <td><%= job.req_number %></td>
48        <td><%= link_to job.title, job %></td>
49        <td><%= job.city %>, <%= job.state %></td>
50
51        <% if current_user && current_user.role == "Admin" %>
52          <td><%= job.job_applications.count if job.job_applications %
            ></td>
53          <td><%= link_to '<i class="fa fa-pencil-square"></i>'.
            html_safe, edit_job_path(job) %></td>
54          <td><%= link_to '<i class="fa fa-minus-square"></i>'.
            html_safe, job, method: :delete, data: { confirm: 'Are
            you sure?' } %></td>
55        <% end %>
56      </tr>
57    <% end %>
```

In this code, the `jobs` instance variable stores a list of jobs and during every iteration, that particular element of `jobs` is stored in the block variable `job`. I can do anything I want with the `job` variable inside my code block. In this example, I'm printing out different elements associated with a specific job.

So, that's how you use the `each` loop in a real-life application.

Now let's take a look at another example that uses the `each` loop. We're going to recreate the max method in Ruby. This method finds the largest value in an array:

```
def new_max array_of_elements
  max_value = 0
  array_of_elements.each do |i|
    if i > max_value
      max_value = i
    end
  end

  max_value
end
```

The `new_max` method leverages the `each` block to loop through a collection of integers by inspecting each element in an array and if it finds a larger value, it updates the `max_value` variable. Once again, this is a nice syntax for looping over a collection because it doesn't force us to know the total number of elements in an array prior to running the script.

The for...in loops tutorial

If you're coming from other programming languages, you may already be familiar with the `for` loops. Ruby also has these types of loops; however, they are not used frequently in real-world applications. This is mainly because the `each` loop is more popular and easier to work with.

With that being said, it's still good to learn about the `for` loops to know all your available options provided in the language. Also, in this lesson, I'm going to show you an easy way to create an array of integers.

The syntax for a `for...in` loop is:

```
for i in 0...42
  p i
end
```

If you run this program, your output should look like this:

In the code, i is our iterator variable, and its value starts at 0. The 0...42 collection is a shortened way of creating an array of integers, and essentially, we are asking the i variable to iterate through this collection and print its own value.

So, this is how you can use the for...in loops to iterate through collections in Ruby.

Looping over a hash

In this section, we are going to walk through how to build a nested iterator with a practical example, namely looping over a nested hash in Ruby.

Before we move on, I'd like to warn you that you have to be careful while working with nested iterators because they can cause performance issues if poorly implemented. If you are working on a collection within another collection, you will go through all the elements in the nested collection when an element of the parent collection is called. This means you will go through a large number of iterations that can potentially slow your program down by quite a bit. Sometimes, the program may even crash if you have to iterate through thousands of elements across multiple collections. So be careful while using these nested iterators.

Nested iterator code example

For our code example, we are going to iterate over a hash data set. You will learn about hashes in-depth in future lessons, but for now, just know that hashes are a key/value-based data structure. Here is a basic nested hash:

```
teams = {
  "Houston Astros" => {
    "first base" => "AJ Reed",
    "second base" => "Jose Altuve",
    "shortstop" => "Carlos Correa"
  },
  "Texas Rangers" => {
    "first base" => "Prince Fielder",
    "second base" => "R. Odor",
    "shortstop" => "Elvis Andrus"
  }
}
```

This is a nested key/value pair structure where we have a collection called `teams`. There are two teams inside this collection, namely, `Houston Astros` and `Texas Rangers`. Inside each of these teams, there are positions and players.

Our program is going to go into the `teams` collection and will iterate over individual positions in each team.

Use the regular `each` loop like this:

```
teams.each do |team|
  p team
end
```

Your output will be as follows:

If you notice, this code prints out all the elements inside each of the two teams. This is great if you just want to see what's inside each element, but if you want to do something with each of the nested elements, then this won't help.

To access the individual elements, we not only have to iterate through the `teams` collection but also through each of the teams present inside this collection. To do that, let's update the code like this:

```ruby
teams.each do |team, players|
  puts team
  players.each do |position, player|
    p "#{player} starts at #{position}"
  end
end
```

In this code, we have two iterator variables for our parent collection, which are `team` and `players`. It's set up this way because we have a collection nested inside another one. In the nested iterator loop, we iterate through the individual team and print out the position and the player. If you see, the nested iterator also has two variables because we have this information in our `players` block variable.

Block variables can be collections as well as single values. When you run into this scenario, it's standard to give a plural name for the block variable, like I did for `players`.

If you run this code, this will be your output:

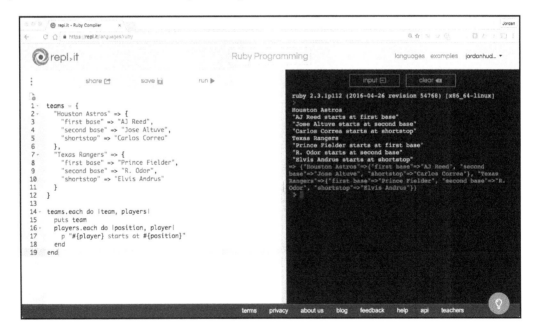

The name of the team gets printed first, and it is followed by the names of the position and players inside each team. Essentially, this code iterated through the `teams` collection, and for every item in the `teams` collection, it displays the elements present in it.

So, this is a practical way of how you can use nested iterators in Ruby to loop through a `Hash` data structure.

Let's take a step back and review another example of how to leverage the `each` method to loop over a key/value hash. We're going to cover hashes in detail later on in the book, for now, just know that hashes are collections, much like arrays. The main difference is that each array element contains an index and a value, whereas hash elements contain a key and a value. Thankfully, the `each` method is smart enough to know when it is looping over an array compared with a hash, and it changes its behavior accordingly. For example, if you attempt to loop over a basic array, your `each` block will only contain one block variable:

```
teams = ['Astros', 'Yankees', 'Rangers']
teams.each do |team|
  puts team
end
```

As you can see, this code has a single block variable that gives you access to each element in the array. Compare this code with what happens when you use the `each` method to loop over a hash:

```
teams = {'AL West': 'Astros', 'AL East': 'Yankees', 'AL Central': 'Royals'}
teams.each do |division, team|
  p "#{team} in the #{division}"
end
```

From this code you can observe that, even though we're using the same `each` method, we can now pass two block variables—one that represents the key, the other represents the value in the collection. You can see that the output will result in the following:

```
"Astros in the AL West"
"Yankees in the AL East"
"Royals in the AL Central"
```

Using the select method

The `select` method is a powerful method that automatically iterates through a collection in a Ruby program and extracts the values you want to retrieve. Enumerators are a fun and powerful way of working with collections in Ruby, and after you get used to implementing the methods, you'll be shocked at how efficient it is to integrate advanced functionality with a limited amount of code.

Before going into the section, I'm going to ask you a question. Say, you are given an array of integers and want to grab only the even integers. How can you do that in Ruby?

If you're coming from other programming languages, you would probably use a `while` loop to iterate through each element, and would check if that element meets the condition of being an even integer.

However, in Ruby, we don't have to go through all that trouble because we can use the `select` method.

To illustrate this functionality, our code will look something like this:

```ruby
(1...10).to_a.select do |x|
  x.even?
end
```

If you run this code, the output will be as follows:

In the preceding code, we are converting a range of integers into an array, running it through the `select` method, and displaying only the even values.

An even better way to do this would be putting this code on one line, like this:

```
(1...10).to_a.select  { |x| x.even?}
```

If you run this, it will give the same output as earlier.

But we're not done yet! Ruby gives us the ability to shorten this code even further, like this:

```
(1...10).to_a.select(&:even?)
```

Since you're likely to see all of these different options in a real-world Ruby project, it's a good idea for you to learn various processes to achieve the same functionality.

If this code looks a little intimidating, don't let it scare you off. In this code, `&` is a shortcut that lets us avoid using a block variable. Whenever we use the `&` syntax, Ruby knows that we want to apply whatever method we are calling to each element in the collection. In our example, we're calling the `even?` method.

Since many professional Ruby developers use the shortcut syntax, you're likely to see the `&` code quite often in production programs.

Let's now examine a few more examples of `select`:

Imagine that we have a sentence or an array of words and want to return only those words that have more than five letters. For this, we are going to use a new type of array syntax.

```
arr = %w(The quick brown fox jumped over the lazy dog)
```

Ruby converts this sentence into an array of words when you precede it with the `%w` symbol. If you just run this code, your output should be:

```
["The", "quick", "brown", "fox", "jumped", "over", "the", "lazy", "dog"]
```

If you notice, the sentence is converted into an array of words.

Now, let's see how we can select on our array to pull out the words with more than five characters:

```
arr = %w(The quick brown fox jumped over the lazy dog)
arr.select { |x| x.length> 5}
```

We cannot use the & block here because we are not calling a standalone method, rather we are running a comparison and this needs a variable.

In the preceding code, I'm checking if the length of each element in the collection is greater than 5, and if so, I'm returning that element. So, my output should be as shown here:

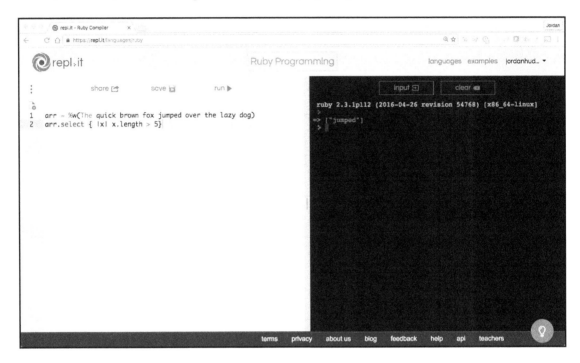

There was only one word that had more than five letters, and that was displayed.

Before we end this section, let's look at one last example. Say, we have a sentence and want the program to return only the vowels. To do that, we can implement the following code:

```
%w(a b c d e f g).select { |v| v =~ /[aeiou]/ }
```

We'll be getting into how to use regular expressions in a later section, so for now, just examine what's going on here in terms of the functionality. Essentially, I'm asking Ruby to pick only the letters that match the vowel list enclosed inside my square brackets. To do this, Ruby will create an array of letters, iterate through each of them, store that item in the v variable, and finally, run a pattern recognition process to see if it matches with the list given inside the square brackets. If it matches, it returns that letter.

If you run this code, the output will be:

Let's take a closer look at how we can pass multiple conditions to the `select` statement:

```ruby
arr = (1..100)
arr.select do |e|
  e % 3 == 0 && e % 5 == 0
end
```

In this code, we're using the modulus operator to extract all of the numbers that are divisible by both 3 and 5. We're going to spend more time learning about conditionals later on in the book; however, this is a good introduction for analyzing how to pass multiple value checks to the `select` method. The result of this code will be this:

```ruby
[15, 30, 45, 60, 75, 90]
```

In this section, you learned four different ways to use the `select` method. I hope this gave you a glimpse into the power of the `select` statement and functional programming in Ruby.

Using the map method – part 1

In the next few sections, we are going to cover the `map` method, which is a popular iteration method used by Ruby developers on a regular basis due to its flexibility and usefulness.

For this guide, I'm going to use the `irb` environment to show you the different environments available for Ruby. If you want to use this environment too, simply type `irb` in your Terminal. Alternatively, you can also use `repl.it` if you prefer.

This is how you can access **Interactive Ruby Shell (irb)**:

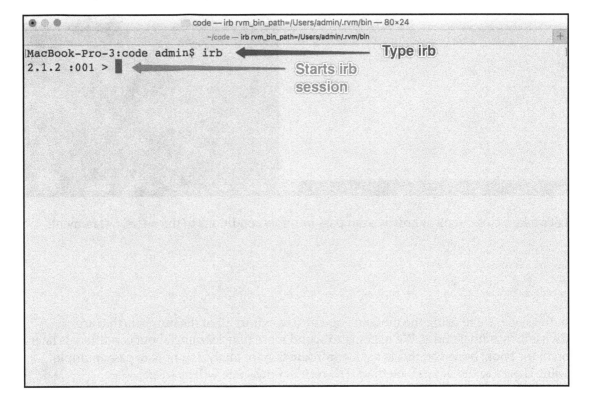

The map method code example

You are going to learn how to use the `map` method with a practical example. Let's imagine that we have an array of strings that represent numbers. This is a common occurrence in Ruby when you work with APIs since they always return values in a string format (even numbers). In cases like these, you may want to convert the values into actual integer data types so that you can use them in your application. This is a great example of how you can leverage the `map` method. Let's enter this code into the `irb` session:

```
["1", "23.0", "0", "4"].map {|x| x.to_i}
```

In this code, we have an array of strings that represent numbers. To convert each value to its integer equivalent, we're using an x block variable and passing the `to_i` method that converts each element to an integer. The output will be as shown here:

```
MacBook-Pro-3:code admin$ irb
2.1.2 :001 > ["1", "23.0'", "0", "4"].map {|x| x.to_i}
 => [1, 23, 0, 4]
2.1.2 :002 > █
```

If you remember our section on the `select` method (*Using the select method*) you will remember that Ruby allows us to use the ampersand shortcut in cases like these. To leverage this syntactic sugar, we can use the following code:

```
["1", "23.0", "0", "4"].map(&:to_i)
```

Running this you'll see that we will get the same result:

```
● ● ●              code — irb rvm_bin_path=/Users/admin/.rvm/bin — 80×24
                   ~/code — irb rvm_bin_path=/Users/admin/.rvm/bin                    +
MacBook-Pro-3:code admin$ irb
2.1.2 :001 > ["1", "23.0'", "0", "4"].map {|x| x.to_i}
 => [1, 23, 0, 4]
2.1.2 :002 > ["1", "23.0", "0", "4"].map(&:to_i)
 => [1, 23, 0, 4]
2.1.2 :003 > █
```

Another example of the `map` method in action would be to double the string value. Let's say you have a list of letters such as a, b, c, and d and you want to double each string, resulting in aa, bb, cc, and dd. This is similar to what you may have seen in an Excel spreadsheet for representing columns.

To accomplish this feature, we can use the following code:

```
("a"..."g").map { |i| i * 2 }
```

In this code, we are declaring a collection that comprises the letters a to g.

 The preceding notation is enough for Ruby to understand that the collection should start from a and end at g and leverages the same range functionality we've used with integers.

Inside of the map block, we're declaring a block variable of i and multiplying each element by two. When you multiply a letter by 2 in Ruby, it simply doubles the letter. So, the output is as shown here:

```
["aa", "bb", "cc", "dd", "ee", "ff"]
```

Let's take a look at one another example with the map method. This time, we are going to convert an array of numbers into a hash that has the key as the number itself and the value as the integer value of the number. If that sounds complicated, don't worry, I simply want to illustrate the power of the method, we can worry about what it means later on when we dive into the Hash data structure.

This is what the code will look like:

```
Hash[[1, 2.1, 3.33, 0.9].map {|x| [x, x.to_i]}]
```

In this code, I'm creating a Hash data structure first. Next, I'm iterating through an array of numbers and mapping it to the hash with the map method. I'm using an x iterator variable to go through each array value. Next, I'm giving two values to the hash, where the first is the value itself, and second is the integer of that value. For example, if a number is 3.33, then the key is 3.33 and value is the integer value of it, which is 3.

This what the output looks like:

```
{1=>1, 2.1=>2, 3.33=>3, 0.9=>0}
```

If you want to have the integer as the key and the actual number as the value, simply switch it up to look like this:

```
Hash[[1, 2.1, 3.33, 0.9].map {|x| [x.to_i, x]}]
```

This will result in the following output:

```
{1=>1, 2=>2.1, 3=>3.33, 0=>0.9}
```

So, in this guide we've walked through three different ways to use the map method. In the next section, we'll discuss the more advanced components that map provides.

Using the map method – part 2

In this section, we are going to go much deeper into the `map` method and explore practical ways of using it in real-world applications.

I'm going to start by reviewing the last example we did in the previous section. In this script, we created a hash from an array of numbers. However, in our example, we're going to build in some custom behavior. We are going to convert a sentence into an array of words and create a hash that takes each word as the key and the length of each word as its corresponding value. The code for this will be as follows:

```
Hash[ %w(A dynamic open source programming language).map { |x| [x,
x.length] } ]
```

If we execute this code, the first hash element should be the word and its corresponding value should be the length of the word. Let's see the output:

```
{"A"=>1, "dynamic"=>7, "open"=>4, "source"=>6, "programming"=>11,
"language"=>8}
```

This worked perfectly. The first key is A and its value, which is the length, is 1. The second key is `dynamic` and its value is 7, the third value is `open` and its value is 4, and so on.

Next, we are going to see how you can use the `map` method in a real-world application, so you know where and how to use it.

If you go to `google.com` and try to search for a keyword such as `ruby programming language`, the URL would be something like this:
`https://google.com/?qws_rd=ssl#safe=off&q=ruby+programming+language`.

Now, what happens if you remove the & and + values from the URL?

If you tried to pass these values into an API as an HTTP request, (something you'll do regularly when building Rails applications), this would throw an error.

In a real-world application, imagine that you get a value that comes in as individual words. You would want to combine them together with the & character to get a URL safe string. We are going to do exactly this using our `map` method.

For example, let's say we have a set of hash values, namely `foo` and `bar`, that have the keys a and b, respectively. To combine them into a safe URL, we can use this code:

```
{:a =>"foo", :b =>"bar"}.map {|a,b| "#{a}=#{b}" }.join('&')
```

In this code, I'm creating a hash with the symbol using the curly bracket syntax and I am using two variables to iterate through the collection. The first a variable is the key while the second b variable is the value. After stringing them together with the = sign, I'm using the & symbol as a string here that joins the next set of values in the hash.

If you hit, your output should be:

```
"a=foo&b=bar"
```

Now lets take a look at another example of how to use the map method. We're going to build a method that generates a flexible baseball lineup. When I say flexible, I mean that the lineup should be able to generate an HTML version, a numbered version, and a bullet point version. So how exactly can a single method be so flexible? We're going to leverage the map method to make it possible. Here is the code that will make it possible:

```
def lineup_generator(list, &block)
  list.map.with_index(1) do |player, index|
    yield(index, player)
  end
end
```

The following array of players is given:

```
players = ['Altuve', 'Correa', 'Bregman']
```

By leveraging the map method combined with a block, we can fulfill all of the requirements by passing in custom block parameters:

```
lineup_generator(@players) { |x, y| "#{x}. #{y}" }
# ["1. Altuve", "2. Correa", "3. Bregman"]

lineup_generator(@players) { |x, y| "<p>#{x}</p> <div>#{y}</div>" }
# ["<p>1</p> <div>Altuve</div>", "<p>2</p> <div>Correa</div>", "<p>3</p>
<div>Bregman</div>"]

lineup_generator(@players) { |x, y| "<li>#{y}</li>" }
# ["<li>Altuve</li>", "<li>Correa</li>", "<li>Bregman</li>"]
```

How is this all possible? The map method allows you to iterate through a collection of data and utilizing the block's yield syntax, we were able to wrap any components needed around each element. Hopefully, this illustrates the power of blocks combined with functional programming in Ruby.

So now you know a number of practical ways to utilize the map method in Ruby programs.

Summing values in an array using the inject method

In this section, I'm going to examine how to sum up values in Ruby by implementing the `inject` method. Being able to sum up values in an array is something you will most likely need in a number of different situations. Thankfully, Ruby makes this very straightforward to implement.

Before we see how to implement the `inject` method, I think it's beneficial to review how to generate a sum manually:

```
total = 0

[3, 2, 4, 53, 5, 3, 23343, 4342, 12, 3].each do |i|
  total += i
end

puts total
```

When you run this program, it will generate the value `27700`, which is the sum of all the individual values present in the array.

However, that took four lines of code. To shorten it, we can use the `inject` method:

```
[3, 2, 4, 53, 5, 3, 23343, 4342, 12, 3].inject(&:+)
```

In this code, we are calling the `inject` method and passing it to each element in the array. The `inject` method is similar to `map` or `select` in the way that it looks at each element in a collection. However, it differs in the sense that it keeps track of the variable value with each iteration. This makes it possible to easily increment all values in a collection and is thus perfect for creating sums.

But `inject` is not limited to creating sums. If we want to multiply all of the values in a collection we can replace + with *:

```
[3, 2, 4, 53, 5, 3, 23343, 4342, 12, 3].inject(&:*)
```

So how exactly was it this easy? It's because + is not an operator in Ruby, rather it is a method. In other programming languages, the parser interprets these symbols as operators, but Ruby treats it as a method and sends it to each of the values of the collection it's iterating through.

With a basic level of `inject` knowledge in place, let's take a look at what else `inject` can do. Because of how the `inject` method works, in addition to summing values, a common pattern you will see in Ruby programs is using `inject` in order to build a new data structure. Let's walk through a practical example. Imagine a situation where you're given an array of integers and you're asked to build a histogram of how many times each integer occurs in the array. A base case example is when you were given an array such as this:

```
[1, 4, 1, 3, 2, 1, 4, 5, 4, 4, 5, 4]
```

The expected histogram needs to be a key/value hash that looks like this:

```
{
    1=>3,
    4=>5,
    3=>1,
    2=>1,
    5=>2
}
```

Notice how each integer listed in the array is counted and the left-hand side represents the integer and the right-hand side counts the number of times that the integer appears in the array? So how can we leverage the `inject` method to build this? Let's create a method called `histogram` and build in the functionality:

```
def histogram nums
  nums.inject(Hash.new(0)) do |hash, e|
    hash[e] += 1
    hash
  end
end
```

Notice how we're using the `inject` method slightly differently from earlier? In this example, we pass in an empty hash as an argument to the method. This will make the default incrementor a hash instead of the integer value of `0`. So instead of summing up or multiplying values, this will allow us to populate a hash with the values we want to pass into it.

Additionally, notice how there are now two block variables? The `inject` method allows us to utilize two block variables, the first one is the incrementor value, which in this case is the `hash`. The second block variable is the current value that is being processed. Inside of the block, we're incrementing the values of each key based on how many times it appears in the hash with the line:

```
hash[e] += 1
```

From that point, we simply return the hash itself so that the `inject` method can continue to use it. The end result will be a hash that counts each of the integers in any array.

So, this is how easy it is to generate a sum from values in an array in Ruby.

Summary

In this chapter, you were introduced to basic looping in Ruby. This chapter discussed the `while` loop, which is a low level iteration mechanism, the `each` loop, which is one of the more common looping tools in programs, and the `for...in` loops in Ruby. We saw how to iterate a key/value hash.

We examined how to utilize the enumerable `select` method and learned three different ways to use the `select` method.

You learned about the `map` method and how it can be utilized to change each element of a collection. We also walked through three different ways to use the `map` method and some of the more advanced components that `map` provides.

Lastly, this chapter walked us through how you can leverage the `inject` method to perform calculations on each element in an array while keeping track of the accumulated value.

In the next chapter, we'll examine the array data structure.

7
Ruby Collections

Nearly every application that you will build will need to implement collections of data in some form or another. This could be anything from a database query that returns multiple records to a set of dates in a calendar. In this chapter, we're going to walk through how to work with collections in a Ruby program, including arrays and hashes. After going through this chapter, you will be able to do the following:

- Demonstrate how to work with data collections in Ruby
- Explain how to work with the array and hash data structures and how to add, edit, and remove items from collections

Using arrays

We're finally getting to work with collections in Ruby! We're going to start with the array data type. In Ruby, arrays are a common data structure that can be utilized in Ruby programs to store a collection of data types, including integers, floats, strings, and even other arrays. We have used arrays quite a bit already in this course. So, in this section, I want to take a step back and walk through some foundational concepts of arrays.

There are two traditional ways to create an array of elements. The first one is to list out a number of elements, surrounded by brackets, and store the array in a variable. In this first example, we're storing five integers in a variable called x:

```
x = [12, 3, 454, 234, 234]
```

Though this is the most common way to create an array, there is also another way to do it, which is to use the `Array.new` syntax, as shown here:

```
y = Array.new
y[0] = 543
```

This will create an array, store it in the variable y, and then add the value of 543 as the zeroth element in the collection.

Arrays have a different numbering system, they start counting from 0 instead of 1.

Now suppose that I want to add a value to the tenth element in the array and remember that since arrays start with an index of 0; this means that there will be 11 elements in the collection. You can accomplish this with the following code:

```
y[10] = 432
```

If I print y, my output will be as shown here:

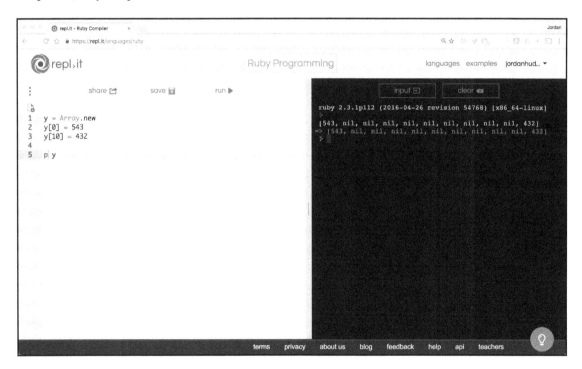

As you can see, our zeroth element is 543 and tenth element is 432, but the remaining values are nil—this is because we haven't filled them. So, you need to keep in mind that an array will fill empty spots if you don't provide the values for them.

To iterate over an array that we create, we can use the `each` iterator method:

```
y.each do |i|
   puts i
end
```

The output will be as follows:

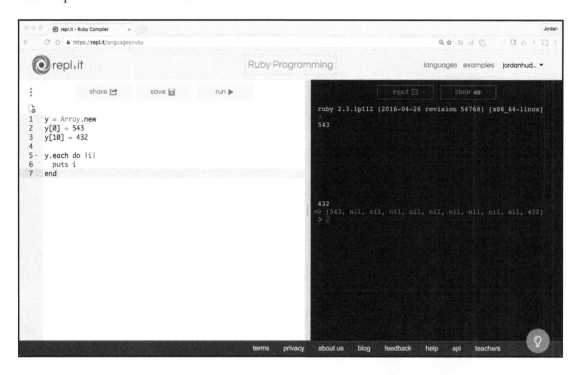

So now you have a good understanding of how to create an array data structure, how to add values to the array, and how to iterate through the collection.

Deleting items from arrays

Now that we know how to create an array and add elements to it, we will now see how to delete items from an array.

Let's start by creating an array. In Ruby, an array can contain elements of different data types, so let's build an array that contains strings, integers, and Booleans:

```
x = ["asdf", 3, 4, 12, "asdf", "b", true, 34, 2, 4, 4, 4]
```

If we want to delete all the 4 elements from the array, we can run the following code:

```
x.delete(4)
```

If we print x, we can see all elements except the 4 elements.

You can check the length of the array before and after deleting all the 4 elements. When you place x.length before the delete method, your array will return a value of 12. Also, if you run the length method after deleting the values of 4, your array's length will only be 8.

Now if I want to remove the element 12, which is the third element in the array now, I can delete it with the following code:

```
x.delete_at(2)
```

 The element 12 was the third element in the array after removing the 4 elements from the array. Also remember that arrays start by counting at 0.

An important item to understand when using the delete_at method is that when you use this method, it not only deletes 12 but also returns it. So, if you ever need the value of the element that was deleted from the array, you can get it from this method. In fact, this is a practical function that you are sure to use while creating applications.

For example, if you want to store a value that was removed from the array, I can do something like this.

```
y = x.delete_at(4)
```

Now, the y variable will have the true value even if this value is no longer present in the array.

There is one more way to delete an element based on a specific condition. Let's examine it with a real-world example:

```
batting_averages = [0.3, 0.18, 0.22, 0.25]
```

Now, if I want to delete all the values that are under a certain average, I can run the code as follows:

```
batting_averages.delete_if { |average| average <0.24}
```

In this code, I'm using a function called `delete_if`, which takes a block. Essentially, this iterates through the array with the `average` block variable, and it will delete all the values that are less than `0.24`. So, my output should only have two elements left in the array, which are, `0.3` and `0.25`.

So, these are the different ways to delete elements from an array.

Using push and pop for arrays

A popular way to work with arrays is to push and pop elements. If you've never heard these terms, let's walk through some basic definitions:

- Pushing is when you add an element to the end of the array
- Popping is when you remove the last item from the array

These processes are similar to inserting and deleting items, except that the behavior occurs at the end of the array.

Let's walk through these processes with some practical examples. I'm going to start by creating an array with the names of baseball teams:

```
teams = ["astros", "yankees", "rangers", "mets", "cardinals"]
```

Now, if I want to push `marlins` (which will add the `marlins` string to the array), I can do it with the following code:

```
teams.push("marlins")
```

If you check the elements in our `teams` array, you can see that `marlins` has been added as the last value. I can also push multiple items in the same code, as follows:

```
teams.push("red sox", "blue jays")
```

These values are added to the end of the array, as you can see here:

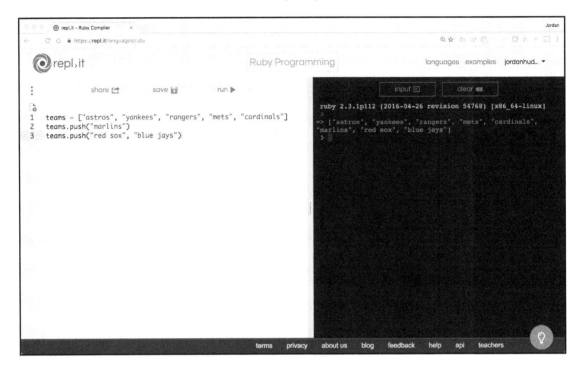

To pop (also known as remove items) items from the end of the array, we can run this simple code:

```
teams.pop
```

If you run this code, the output will be blue jays. If you notice, Ruby returns this value, so you can store it in a variable and run any process you want with it. Consider this example:

```
z = teams.pop
```

Now if you check the value of the z variable, it will have the red sox value:

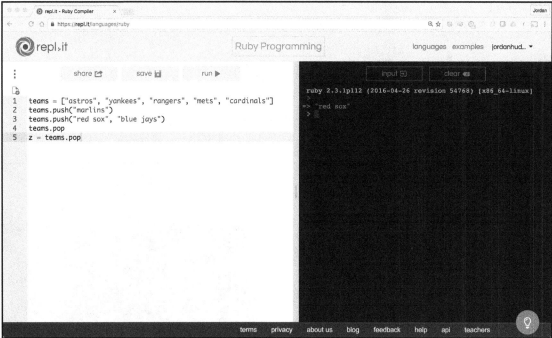

So, that's how you push and pop with Ruby arrays.

The Ruby hash tutorial

For complex collections, the hash data structure is a powerful tool in Ruby programs. Hashes are key/value-based and let you access data elements with more than a pure index, such as with arrays. Though we've briefly touched on hashes in the previous lessons, I want to give you a firm understanding of what hashes are and how they can be used.

Essentially, a hash is a key/value pair collection. In an array, each element is a single item such as a number or word whereas in a hash, each element has two items, and includes a value and a key associated with it.

Sometimes, the value itself can be another collection like an array or a hash.

The hash code example

Let's start by creating a hash:

```
positions = {
            first_base: "Chris Carter",
            second_base: "Jose Altuve",
            short_stop: "Carlos Correa"
       }
```

When you run this code, you can see the hash, where the keys are mapped to their respective values:

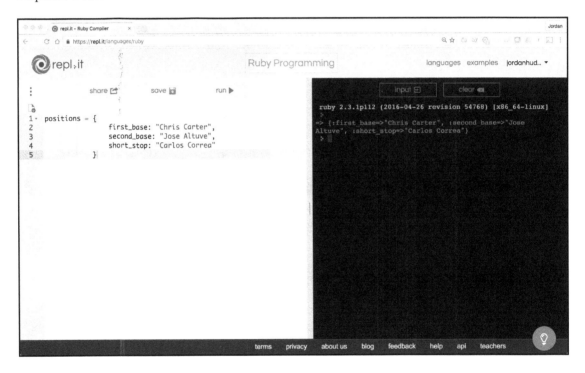

In the written code, I placed each key/value pair on their own line for readability purposes; however, you can also use the `irb` console and build the hash on a single line. This is an important item to know because the Ruby parser doesn't care about white spaces, so both options will work fine. However, when you're building code-based programs it's considered a best practice to place each element on its own line.

If you see the following output you can see that Ruby has automatically inserted a colon in front of every position to denote that it's the key and it is mapped to a value with the `=>` symbol, which is called a **hash rocket**:

```
{:first_base=>"Chris Carter", :second_base=>"Jose Altuve",
:short_stop=>"Carlos Correa"}
```

Though the preceding code is the most modern syntax to create a hash, there are other ways to create one too. It's important to understand the different ways to create a hash, especially, if you're going to be working with existing Ruby applications, since you will most likely see both options in the wild:

```
positions = { "first_base" => "Chris Carter", " second_base" => "Jose
Altuve", "short_stop" => "Carlos Correa" }
```

If you run it, the output will be the same as when we used the first syntax. Another way to create a hash would be this:

```
positions = { :first_base =>"Chris Carter", :second_base =>"Jose Altuve",
:short_stop =>"Carlos Correa" }
```

So, all these three syntaxes will generate the same behavior; which syntax you go with is up to your own preferences. Typically, I utilize the first colon-based version.

Next, let's see how to select an item from a hash that you've created:

```
positions = {
            first_base: "Chris Carter",
            second_base: "Jose Altuve",
            short_stop: "Carlos Correa"
        }

positions[:second_base]
```

If you run this code, you can see that it will output the player name, `Jose Altuve`:

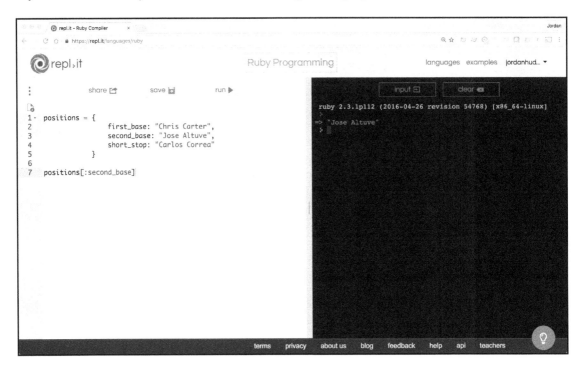

The easy way to remember how to grab items from a hash is that you use the key to look up the corresponding value, and you pass it in as a symbol. This feature is one of the reasons why hashes are so popular for developers. Notice how you don't have the same flexibility with arrays. With arrays, if you want to grab an element from the collection, you either have to know its position in the array or you have to iterate through it until you find the item you want to select.

However, with hashes, we can look up items based on their key, which is more practical in many different cases. Having a clear understanding of the differences between hashes and arrays is important so you can decide when to use each type of data structure.

Now, I'm going to show you what this looks like in a real-life application:

```
1  class JobsController < ApplicationController
2    before_action :set_job, only: [:show, :edit, :update, :destroy]
3    before_action :authenticate_user!, only: [:edit, :new, :destroy]
4
5    # GET /jobs
6    # GET /jobs.json
7    def index
8      @jobs = Job.paginate(page: params[:page], per_page: 10)
9    end
10
```

If you look at the `index` method, you can see that it calls a method called `paginate`. This method allows our application to have pagination links. Looking inside the list of arguments passed to the method you'll see that we're passing a value called `params[:page]`. Does this syntax look familiar? The Ruby on Rails framework stores all of the parameters for a page in a hash structure. By calling `params[:page]`, we can tell our pagination process what page to look for.

I hope this gives you an idea of how to get started with hashes. In the next few guides, we'll explore various ways we can work with this data structure.

Deleting elements from a hash

In this section, we'll examine how to delete items from a Ruby hash. Let's start by creating a new hash called `people`. It will contain the names and ages of people:

```
people = { jordan: 32, tiffany: 27, kristine: 10, heather: 29 }
```

I can confirm that this is working by attempting to select a value using the following code:

```
people[:tiffany]
```

The preceding code will return the value of `27`.

Deleting from a hash is similar to how you would do it from an array, except, instead of an index, we'll pass the key as a symbol:

```
people.delete(:kristine)
```

This method not only deletes that record from the hash but also returns the value, which in this case, is the age of `kristine`.

Now, if you go to the hash, you can see that it has only three key/value pairs instead of the original four, because one was deleted:

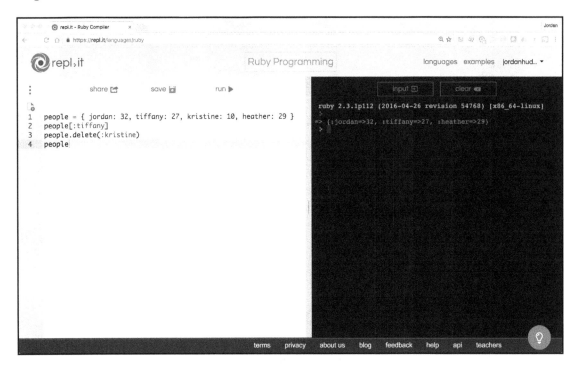

So, that's how you can delete values from a hash.

Iterating over a hash for a key or value

You already learned how to iterate through a hash in one of our previous sections, however, it's a very critical task that you'll be using quite often. With that in mind, I'm going to discuss how it works in more detail. Also, I'm going to show you how you can iterate over only the keys or values.

I'm going to start with the hash we created in the previous section:

```
people = { jordan: 32, tiffany: 27, kristine: 10, heather: 29 }
```

When you want to only grab the keys, your code can be like this:

```
people.each_key do |key|
  puts key
end
```

If I run this code, it prints out each one of the keys like this:

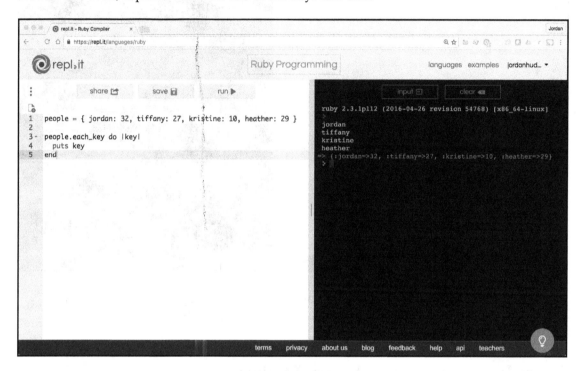

Now, to iterate through the values, we can leverage the `each_value` iterator method, like this:

```
people.each_value do |value|
  puts value
end
```

This will print out the values, which in this case, are the ages of people in the hash:

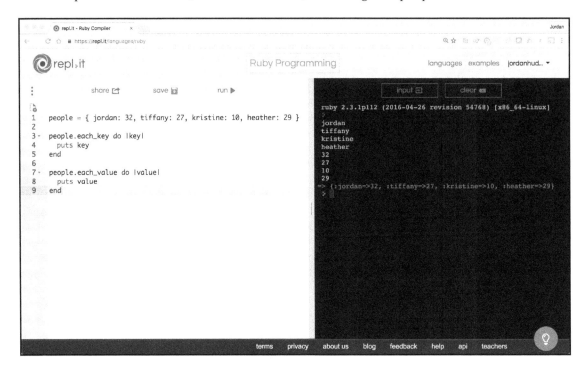

These built-in methods make it easy to isolate the elements that you really care about grabbing from a hash instead of being forced to iterate over both keys and values.

Top hash methods in Ruby

Since hashes are an integral part of Ruby, I want to go through some helpful methods that can be quite handy for development projects.

We are going to use the same `people` hash that we have been working over the last few sections:

```
people = {jordan: 32, tiffany: 27, kristine: 10, heather: 29}
```

Adding elements to a hash

First, we are going to see how to add items to a hash. To do that, add in the following code:

```
people[:leann] = 42
```

Now, if you type `people`, you can see this new element has been successfully added:

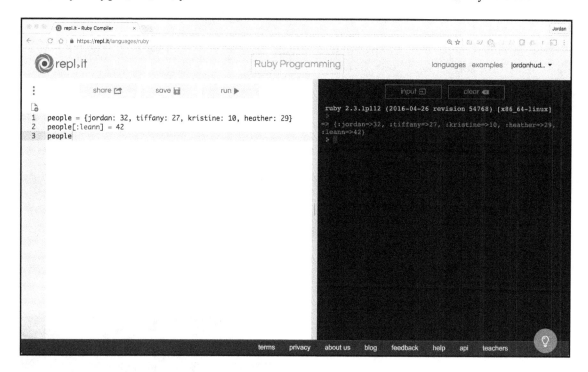

So adding to a hash is similar to adding to arrays. But instead of passing in an index and value, you supply a key and then a value.

Swapping keys and values

Next, we are going to see how to reverse the key/value pair values. For our example, let's imagine that we want to swap out the hash so that the age is the key and the name is the value.

One way to do is to iterate through each pair, store it in a variable, swap them, and update. But, that's slow and more tedious. A better and easier way would be to leverage Ruby's `invert` method:

```
people.invert
```

This does the swapping work for us:

```
{32=>:jordan, 27=>:tiffany, 10=>:kristine, 29=>:heather, 42=>:leann}
```

This method can be particularly useful if you want to store the inverted values into a new hash, which we can do with code, like the following:

```
people_2 = people.invert
```

Merging hashes

Next, we are going to see how to merge the two hashes, `people` and `people_2` together:

```
people.merge(people_2)
```

The output is as follows:

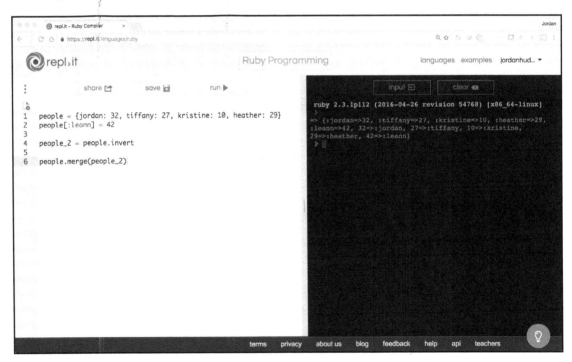

Converting a hash into an array

Next, we are going to see how to convert a hash into an array. We can leverage the built-in Ruby array conversion method to accomplish this for us, as you can see here:

```
Array(people)
```

 Ruby has a number of data type conversion methods. For example, to convert a hash to an array you could use either `Array(people)` or `people.to_a`. The differences are subtle and for the majority of cases, either option will work for your needs.

The output of this code is as follows:

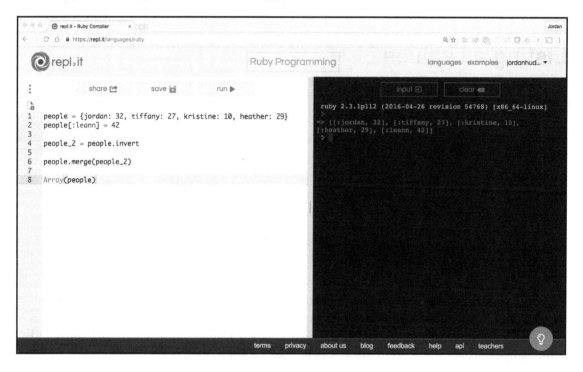

Taking a look at our newly rendered array, each key/value pair has been converted to an array, nested inside one large array that contains all of the pairs. This method gives you the flexibility to swap between an array and a hash based on your program needs.

Listing all keys

So what happens if you want to see all of the keys in a hash? You could iterate through the hash with the `each_key` method that we've used before. However, you can also get the list of keys by simply calling the following method:

```
people.keys
```

This method will list out all of the keys for you and place them into an array:

```
[:jordan, :tiffany, :kristine, :heather, :leann]
```

This is great for debugging; however, if you want to do something with each key, then iterating through the hash with the `each_key` method is most likely a smarter choice.

Listing all values

Similarly, you can see all of the values with the `values` method:

```
people.values
```

Running this code will give the following output:

```
[32, 27, 10, 29, 42]
```

Note that both the `keys` and `values` hash methods return the elements as an array. So if you want to store all the keys or all the values in an array, this is a great way of doing it.

Summary

In this introductory chapter, we analyzed how to work with the array data structure in Ruby and examined three ways to delete items from an array (using the functions `delete`, `delete_at`, and `delete_if`). We examined how Ruby implements the ability to add and remove items from the end of an array using `push` and `pop` methods.

We also discussed how to work with the hash data structure, which enables developers to store key/value-based data, and we analyzed how to remove items from a hash. We also walked through how to iterate through a hash. After going through these sections, you must be able to appreciate how flexible the Ruby programming language is when it comes to working with hashes.

We also examined some of the most beneficial methods you can call on hashes for performing various tasks such as adding to a hash, listing all of the keys and values with a single method call, and merging hashes together.

In the next chapter, we'll start looking at conditionals.

8
Ruby Conditionals

A key component for building dynamic behavior into Ruby applications requires conditional logic at some stage or another. In this chapter, you'll learn how to integrate conditionals into a Ruby program, which will enable your programs to have dynamic behavior based on different input data. After finishing this chapter, you will be able to do the following:

- Demonstrate how to use `if...else` and compound conditionals
- Develop programs with conditional logic in Ruby programs to manage data flow

The conditionals guide

In this section, we are going to talk about conditionals in Ruby. This is a very important component of learning how to code, since conditionals allow our programs to make decisions based on varying data.

Real-world use of conditionals

Imagine that you're building a self-driving car. Your car would have sensors providing information such as GPS coordinates, the location and speed of the vehicles around the car, and the list goes on and on.

All of this data is great; however, how can we use it to make sure our car functions properly? Our program could follow a set of rules—the following are a few basic ones:

- If the speed limit is 40 MPH, ensure to match this speed
- If there is an accident in front of the car, slow down
- If the car has less than 1/4 of fuel then stop at a gas station

Do you notice how each of these requirements evaluates a parameter and changes the behavior of the car based on its value? This is how conditionals work.

At a high-level, conditionals analyze a scenario, compare it with the data provided, and then alter the flow of a program based on the results.

Code example of conditionals

Let's start with the most basic conditional: the standard `if` statement:

```
x = 10
y = 5

if x == y
  puts "x is the same as y"
else
  puts "x and y are not the same"
end
```

If you run this code, the message is `x and y are not the same`.

If I change the value of `x` to `5` and run it, the message is `x is the same as y`.

Do you see how you can almost read the code like plain language? This easy-to-read syntax is one of the reasons so many developers have fallen in love with Ruby. This conditional can be read as follows:

If `x` is equal to `y`, print `x is the same as y`, else, print `x and y are not the same`.

In the next sections, we'll walk through how we can implement conditionals into programs and give dynamic behavior to programs.

Syntax for the unless conditional

The `unless` conditional is a popular programming process for many *Rubyists*. It's not required and many developers I know, even experienced ones, don't like it since it is a very different way of looking at conditionals. I'll leave it up to you to decide if you feel good about using it in your own programs. Either way, you'll run into it in a large number of Ruby programs, so it's important to at least understand the syntax.

Running Ruby files

In this section, I'm going to use a regular Ruby file because I want you to get familiar with the different environments to write and execute Ruby code. As a quick review, to run Ruby code inside files, you can carry out the following steps:

1. Create a file with a text editor or IDE, making sure the file ends in .rb.
2. Open up the Unix Terminal and make sure that you're in the same directory as the file that you created. If you're new to using the Terminal, you can save your file to the Desktop and then direct your Terminal to the Desktop with the cd ~/Desktop command.
3. From here, you can run the Ruby file with the following Terminal command:

```
ruby name_of_your_file.rb
```

The unless conditional code example

In working through the unless conditional, I created a file called unless_syntax.rb.

First, I create an array for our unless conditional to work with:

```
players = ["Correa", "Carter", "Altuve"]
```

I want my code to print the values from the players array, but only if the array has values in it. To accomplish this, I'm going to use the following code:

```
unless players.empty?
  players.each{ |player| puts player }
end
```

To run this program, go to the Terminal and type ruby unless_syntax.rb.

The output is as follows:

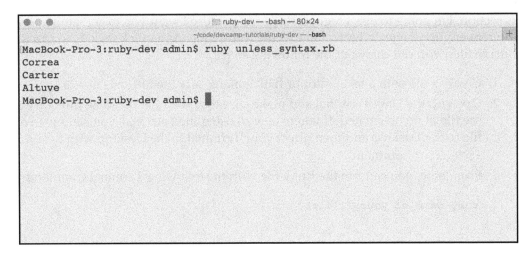

Now, what happens if the array is empty?

Remove the values from the array as shown in the following code:

```
players = []

unless players.empty?
  players.each{ |player| puts player }
end
```

Save the file and run it in the Terminal. The following is the output that you will see:

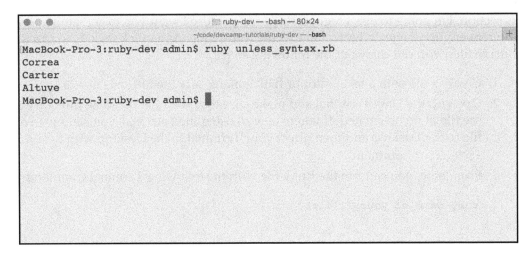

The program doesn't print anything because this is following the rule that our `unless` conditional dictated. Now if you're a natural born skeptic like me you may say, "nothing got printed because nothing was in the array!" Fair enough; let's update the code to look like this:

```
players = []

unless players.empty?
  puts "I'm inside the unless statement"
  players.each { |player| puts player }
end
```

Now if you run this code, you'll see that nothing gets printed. Even `"I'm inside the unless statement"` isn't shown. This is because the way that conditionals work is that they check to see if the condition is met, and if it's not (like our `players` array being empty), it will skip all of the code inside of the `unless` block.

If you read the code like spoken language, it should read like the following:

Unless the `players` array is empty, print it out.

In the second run, the `players` array was empty, so the program does not process the code in the block.

Now the `unless` conditional can be challenging for some developers to get their mind around. Essentially, `unless` is the exact opposite of `if`. For example, we could change our program to say `if !players.empty?`, and it would work the same as our current code which is based on `unless`.

You can use either option depending on what you prefer. Personally, there are a number of circumstances when `unless` makes sense to use, so I utilize it in those cases.

In the preceding example, we used `unless` with a code block. However, I'll typically use `unless` on a single line of code. For example, we can refactor our code to read like the following:

```
players.each{ |player| puts player } unless players.empty?
```

This is one of the nicest things about Ruby because you can actually read this one line of code like a spoken sentence:

Iterate through each value in the `players` array and print each player unless the array is empty.

How simple is that! Not all programming languages offer this type of convenience. I can also do the same thing with the `if` statement too (assuming I use the `!` process to get the opposite value):

```
players.each{ |player| puts player } if !players.empty?
```

I hope this helps you to appreciate the simplicity of Ruby and the flexibility it gives you to utilize multiple syntax options to accomplish the same behavior.

Nested if...else conditionals

In this section, we are going to extend our knowledge of conditionals by learning about the `if...elsif` mechanism. This tool allows us to set up multiple conditional scenarios for our programs to manage data flow. Ruby has a slightly odd syntax on this functionality, so let's walk through it one step at a time.

The if...elsif conditional code example

To review, I'm going to start off with a regular `if` statement:

```
x = 10
y = 100
z = 10

if x == y
  puts "x is equal to y"
end
```

If you run this program, nothing will print out since x is not equal to y. This is what you already know. Now, I'm going to add some additional scenarios:

```
if x == y
  puts "x is equal to y"
elsif x > z
  puts "x is greater than z"
else
  puts "Something else"
end
```

Essentially, this code is going to check if x is equal to y, and if it's not, it moves down to the next condition and checks if x is greater than z, which if not true again means that, it finally prints Something else. Whenever you have an else statement in a program like this, it will be treated like a fallback value, which means that it will be processed if none of the conditionals above it were true.

Now, if I make a small change and alter the elsif statement to read x is greater than or equal to z, then my output should be x is greater than or equal to z:

```
if x == y
  puts "x is equal to y"
elsif x >= z
  puts "x is greater than or equal to z"
else
  puts "Something else"
end
```

The conditional workflow

In these multiple if...else conditionals, Ruby moves in a sequential order from one condition to the other. When any particular condition is satisfied, it does the following:

- Enters that code block
- Performs the logic
- Exits out of the if...else loop

Now, lets' see what happens when more than one condition is true:

```
if x == y
  puts "x is equal to y"
elsif x >= z
  puts "x is greater than or equal to z"
elsif x < z
  puts "x is less than y"
else
  puts "Something else"
end
```

In the preceding example, both the elsif statements are true. Still, Ruby will only process the elsif x >= z because it is true. From there, it will simply exit the if...else workflow. So, the output is the same.

This is something that you should keep in mind while creating an if...else statement in Ruby. I've had confusing bugs arise in programs where I couldn't figure out why a program wasn't generating the value I expected. I ended up discovering that a conditional higher up the conditional chain was resolving to a true value and the condition I wanted the program to reach was skipped completely.

Guide to compound conditionals

So far in this section we have seen if, unless, if...else, and if...elsif statements and how they work in Ruby programs. Additionally, there are times when you may want to combine multiple conditionals together to enable a more granular data check. In this guide, I will show you how to utilize multiple conditionals per line.

Compound conditionals code example

Let's say you want to check for two nested conditions. Technically, you could accomplish the desired output with this code:

```
x = 10
y = 100
z = 10

if x == y
  if x == z
    puts "equal to everything"
  end
end
```

This code checks if x and y are the same, and if true, also checks if x and z are the same. If the nested condition is also satisfied, then it prints equal to everything.

Even though this works, it's pretty ugly and could lead to code that's hard to read and debug. Thankfully, there is another way to create the same behavior:

```
if x == y && x == z
  puts "from the if statement"
end
```

If you run this program you'll see nothing gets printed. This is because both the statements are not true, but only one is true. That is, x is not equal to y, but x is equal to z. Since the && symbol means that both statements need to be true, the message was not printed.

Now, if I change `&&` to `||`, then we are asking Ruby to print the message if only one statement is true. In other words, `||` stand for OR while `&&` stands for AND:

```
if x == y || x == z
  puts "from the if statement"
end
```

Since only one condition has to be true, this version of the program will print the text:

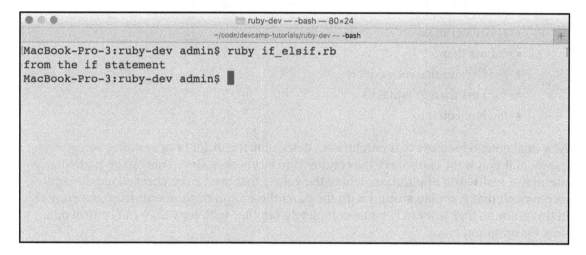

Technically, you can replace the symbols with the `or` and `and` words, but there are some small differences that can throw errors, so I prefer to use the symbols. So, this is how you can implement compound conditionals in Ruby.

Compounded compound conditionals

Ruby doesn't limit you to two conditionals; technically, you can place as many conditions as you want. Consider this example:

```
if (x == 10 && x == z) || x == y
  puts "from the if statement"
end
```

This code will print the statement for you. This is because Ruby follows the order of operations (the same order of operations you learned in `Chapter 04`, *Working with Numbers in Ruby*), so it will check the code within the parentheses first. If this value is true, it sees the `||` statement, and since it already knows that the left side is true, it runs the code inside of the `if` statement.

If you change `||` to `&&`, then nothing gets printed because the second part of the conditional is not true.

Additional conditional operators

In this section, I will primarily use the `==` operator, but you can also use the `>`, `<`, `>=`, `<=`, and `!=` operators in conditionals. These represent the following statements:

- `>`: Greater than
- `<`: Less than
- `>=`: Greater than or equal to
- `<=`: Less than or equal to
- `!=`: Not equal to

As a final note, remember that parentheses determine the order of operations, so you can use them if you want one part of the condition to be checked first. This can be particularly useful in a real-world application, where the values that need to be checked are dynamic. I recommend that you play around with the parentheses and conditionals from the examples in this guide so that you can become completely familiar with how they can control data flow for programs.

Summary

In this chapter, we explored the basic syntax for conditionals in Ruby. Conditionals are one of the building blocks for many programs, so make sure to run through these examples multiple times to familiarize yourself with the keywords. We also analyzed the `unless` conditional, which is essentially the contrapositive of the traditional `if...else` conditional, so it can be confusing to many developers. We saw how to work with nested conditionals. Specifically, we analyzed both the syntaxes and also how conditionals operate from a data flow perspective. This chapter also walked us through how to use compound conditionals in Ruby. Additionally, we defined the list of conditional operators that you can utilize in a program.

In the next chapter, we'll start analyzing object-oriented programming in Ruby.

9
Object-Oriented Programming in Ruby

One of the defining attributes of the Ruby programming language, in addition to readability, is how it implements **object-oriented programming** (**OOP**) techniques. In this chapter, you'll learn OOP for Ruby, including creating classes, instantiating objects, working with inheritance, and polymorphism. Additionally, you'll be able to do the following:

- Work with Ruby classes
- Use getter and setter methods in Ruby
- Demonstrate how to implement OOP techniques such as inheritance and polymorphism
- Employ the SOLID design patterns to follow OOP best practices

Introduction to how OOP works

In this chapter, we are going to look into a fundamental concept called OOP. If you're coming from other OOP languages, you may be familiar with some of these concepts, but still it's important that you pay attention because Ruby embraces a very specific form of OOP compared with many other languages available today.

Before we begin, a key thing to remember is that pretty much of everything is an object in Ruby. We'll see more of it as we go. Also, I'll show some practical ways of using OOP, which hopefully will be more enlightening than the theoretical approach taught in most computer science books. In fact, teaching a practical application of OOP was one of my biggest motivators to create this course.

When I was studying development in college, I thought I learned OOP. However, what I learned in school did little to help me build real-world programs and I ended up having to relearn a practical approach to OOP as I taught myself how to code.

A real-world OOP example

Let's start by analyzing a Ruby on Rails project that I built for a client:

```
 1  class ApplicationController < ActionController::Base
 2
 3
 4    protect_from_forgery unless: -> { request.format.json? }
 5
 6    # include DixieUtils::Authentication
 7
 8
 9    rescue_from CanCan::AccessDenied do |exception|
10      redirect_to :controller =>:pages, :action =>'unauthorised', :alert => except
11    end
12
13    # Prevent CSRF attacks by raising an exception.
14    # For APIs, you may want to use :null_session instead.
15    #protect_from_forgery with: :exception
16
17
18    skip_before_action :verify_authenticity_token
19
20
21  end
22
```

If you see the first line, I have a class called `ApplicationController`, which inherits from a class called `ActionController::Base`. The < symbol denotes inheritance in Ruby.

 Make sure not to get the < symbol used for inheritance confused with the < symbol used with conditionals. The Ruby parser is smart enough to differentiate when you want to use one over the other.

What this code essentially means is that, `ApplicationController` has access to all the methods available in `ActionController::Base`. In this sense, the attributes and behavior of a class are determined largely by the class from which they inherit.

Now, there can be classes that inherit from `ApplicationController`. I'll open another file to show you how this works:

```
1  class BranchesController < ApplicationController
2
3    before_action :set_branch, only: [:show, :edit, :update, :destroy]
4
5    #load_and_authorize_resource
6
7    def index
8      @branches = Branch.all
9      @branch_categories = BranchCategory.all
10     respond_to do |format|
11       format.html
12       format.json { render json: @branches }
13     end
14   end
15
16   def new
17     @branch = Branch.new
18     @branch_categories = BranchCategory.all
19     @managers = Manager.all
20
21     respond_to do |format|
22       format.html{ render 'branches/html/new' }
23     end
24   end
```

Here, the first line tells you that `BranchesController` is a class that inherits from the `ApplicationController`. Due to this inheritance, methods present in `ApplicationController` such as `index` and `new` can be accessed by `BranchesController`. The same applies to the `before_action` method too. I've not declared this method anywhere in `BranchesController`, yet I have access to it because it is present in `ApplicationController`. But wait! There was no mention of these methods inside of `ApplicationController`, so where did these methods come from? Don't worry, it's not coding black magic. These methods are passed down from `ActionController::Base` from which `ActionController` inherits.

If this is still fuzzy, let's think of a real-world example of inheritance. As humans, each of us have biological parents. Our parents passed down a set of genes to us that our bodies have access to. In this analogy, our parents are like the `ActionController::Base` class and we are the `BranchesController` class. The genes that our parents pass to us are like the methods that our `BranchesController` class has access to.

Let's take a look at another code example from the Rails project; let's go to the `create` method in the `BranchController` class:

```
26   def create
27     @branch = Branch.new(branch_params)
28     @managers = Manager.all
29     @branch_categories = BranchCategory.all
30
31     respond_to do |format|
32       if @branch.save
33
34         format.html { redirect_to @branch, notice: 'Branch was successfully gen
35         format.json { render :show, status: :created}
36       else
37         format.html { render 'branches/html/new' }
38         format.json { render json: @branch.errors, status: :unprocessable_entit
39       end
40     end
41
42   end
```

If you see, in line 27, I create a new instance of the class called `Branch` and pass some custom parameters to it. I can access the methods of this `Branch` class through the `branch` instance I created here.

Now, if I go to the `Branch` class, you can see that it inherited from another class called `ActiveRecord::Base`:

```
1   class Branch < ActiveRecord::Base
2     belongs_to :brach_categories, dependent: :destroy
3     belongs_to :manager, foreign_key: :manager_id
4     has_many :business_cards
5     has_many :vender_requests
6     mount_uploader :logo, CorpFileUploader
7     mount_uploader :bg_template, CorpFileUploader
8     mount_uploader :footer_img, CorpFileUploader
9     validates_presence_of :name, :address_one, :city, :state, :zip_code, :logo, :f
10
11
12
13
14    def self.first_approver(branch)
15      branch.manager
16    end
17
18    def self.secnd_approver(branch)
19      branch.manager.name
20    end
21
22  end
```

By inheriting from the `ActiveRecord::Base` class, our `Branch` class will have access to a large number of methods that it can call when it needs them. The methods that our `Branch` class inherit allows it to do the following:

- Communicate with the database
- Implement data validations
- Launch automated processes named callbacks
- And much more

When you get into the Ruby on Rails application development, you'll see inheritance is used extensively.

If you've never worked with OOP before, this all may seem a bit overwhelming; however, don't let it scare you off. I wanted to start by showing you a practical example of how OOP works because I was tired of instructors who gave contrived OOP examples. I'd prefer for you to see what OOP does in a real application so you will realize how important it is.

In the next few guides, we will be building out our own application, which will be an API connector that can communicate dynamically with applications on the web. This will include walking through how to leverage concepts such as inheritance and object instantiation to make our code more scalable and reusable.

Ruby OOP development – setters, getters, and methods

Ruby utilizes a unique syntax for creating setters and getters in a class. In this guide, we will walk through how to implement these processes.

Creating a class is fairly simple in Ruby. It's so simple that it wasn't even worth dedicating an entire guide to it (I build courses just like I code—I despise wasting my time or yours for dead simple concepts).

To define a class simply type the `class` word followed by the name you want to give to your class, and end it with the `end` word. Anything contained between `class` and `end` belongs to this class.

 Class names in Ruby have a very specific style requirement. They need to start with a letter and if they represent multiple words, each new word needs also to be an uppercase letter.

We'll start by creating a class called `ApiConnector`:

```
class ApiConnector
end
```

Now classes in Ruby can store both data and methods. But how can we define what data should be included? In many traditional OOP languages such as Java, you need to create two methods for each data element you want to be included in the class. One method, the **setter**, sets the value in the class. The other method, the **getter**, allows you to retrieve the value.

The process of creating setter and getter methods for every data attribute can be tiresome and leads to incredibly long class definitions. Thankfully Ruby has a set of tools called **attribute accessors**.

Let's implement some setters and getters for some new data elements for our class. Since it's an API connector, it would make sense to have data elements such as `title`, `description`, and `url`. We can add these elements with the following code:

```
class ApiConnector
  attr_accessor :title, :description, :url
end
```

Let's now instantiate this class. We'll have an entire guide dedicated to instantiation since it can be confusing if you've never used it before. At a higher level it means this—I'll create an instance of that class, so that we can use it to do something.

When you merely create a class, it doesn't do anything by itself as it is simply a definition; however, in order to work with the class, we need to create an instance of it. This is just like how a blueprint of a house isn't actually a house, it simply defines what the house will look like. In order to live in the house, you have to build it. Instantiating a class is like building a house based on a blueprint.

This class can be instantiated with this code:

```
api = ApiConnector.new
```

In this code, we create a new instance of the `ApiConnector` class and store it in a variable called `api`.

Now that we have an object created, we can use the `api` variable to work with the class attributes. For example, I can run the code:

```
api.url = "http://google.com/"
puts api.url
```

If you run this file, it will result in the following output:

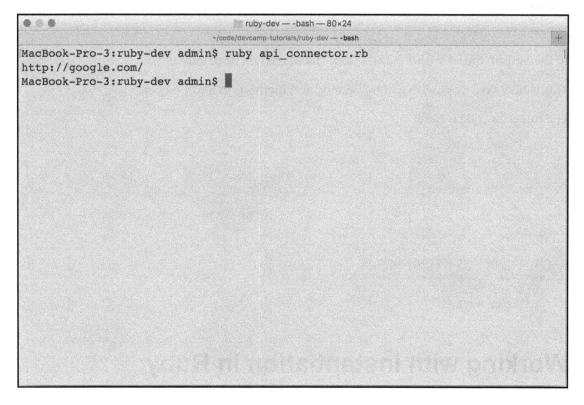

This code is using both the setter and getter methods:

- `api.url = "http://google.com/"`: This is setting the `url` attribute value to `http://google.com/`
- `api.url`: This is getting the value from the class

This is how you create a class and communicate with its data using attribute accessors.

In addition to creating attributes, you can also create methods in a class:

```
def test_method
  puts "testing class call"
end
```

To access this method, we can use the same syntax that we utilized with the attribute accessors:

```
api.test_method
```

In the output, the `testing class call` message will be printed.

This is how you work with getters, setters, and methods in a Ruby class.

The full class code is here:

```
class ApiConnector
  attr_accessor :title ,  :description ,  :url

  def test_method
    puts  "testing class call"
  end
end

api =  ApiConnector .new
api.url =  "http://google.com/"
puts api.url
api.test_method
```

Working with instantiation in Ruby

If you're new to OOP, a natural question to ask is—what does instantiation mean? Like many other concepts in the development world, instantiation is actually a relatively straightforward concept that suffers from having an overly complex name.

What does instantiation mean? – A real-world example

Before we dive into the code, let's analyze a real-world example of instantiation. (A quick spoiler alert. If you understand what it takes to build a house, you already understand instantiation.)

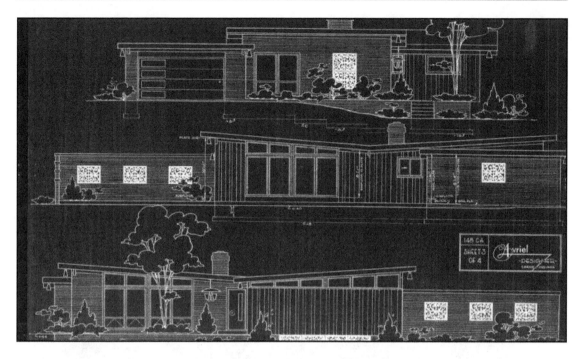

Let's imagine that you're building a house. One of the first tasks you'd most likely do is build a blueprint for the house. This blueprint would contain attributes and features of the house, such as these:

- The dimensions for each room
- How the plumbing will flow
- Essentially, every attribute/feature of the house

Now let me ask a dumb question. Is the blueprint of the house the actual house? No, it simply lists out the attributes and design elements for how the home will be created.

So after the blueprint is completed, the actual home can be built. Dare I say that the home can be instantiated?

Connecting the dots

From an OOP perspective, a **class** is the blueprint for an object. A class simply describes what an object will look like and how it will behave.

Therefore, **instantiation** is the process of taking a class definition and creating an object that you can use in a program.

Still a little fuzzy? That's fine; let's look at a code example.

Instantiation code example

For this example, we will have an `Invoice` class. Inside the class definition, we have attributes, such as a `customer` and `total`, along with some behavior, such as printing out an invoice summary:

```ruby
class Invoice
  attr_accessor:customer, :total

  def summary
    puts "Invoice:"
    puts "Customer: #{customer}"
    puts "Total: #{total}"
  end
end
```

Implementing instantiation

Now that we have our class definition, we can create a new instance of `Invoice` and store it in a variable, as shown here:

```ruby
class Invoice
  attr_accessor :customer, :total

  def summary
    puts "Invoice:"
    puts "Customer: #{customer}"
    puts "Total: #{total}"
  end
end

invoice = Invoice.new
```

I have used instantiation to do the following:

1. Take a class.
2. Build an object based on the class definition.

With this process in place, I can use the object to perform tasks, such as setting the values of the attributes and accessing the methods:

```ruby
class Invoice
  attr_accessor:customer, :total

  def summary
    puts "Invoice:"
    puts "Customer: #{customer}"
    puts "Total: #{total}"
  end
end

invoice = Invoice.new
invoice.customer = "Google"
invoice.total = 500
invoice.summary
```

Running this code will give us the following output:

```
Invoice:
Customer: Google
Total: 500
```

At its core, instantiation is the process of taking a class, and creating an object from it that you can actually use in your program.

Creating an initializer method in a Ruby class

One thing you may find handy in Ruby development is to create an initializer method. If you're wondering what is an initializer method, it is simply a method called `initialize` that will run every time when you create an instance of your class. In this method, you can give values to your variables, call other methods, and do just about anything that you think should happen when a new instance of that class is created.

If you're coming from other languages, this initializer method is similar to a constructor.

Adding an initializer to a Ruby class

Let's update our `ApiConnector` class to utilize an initializer method.

This update class will look something like the following:

```
class ApiConnector
  def initialize(title, description, url)
    @title = title
    @description = description
    @url = url
  end
end
```

For now, I'm creating an instance variable for each of my parameters so that I can use these variables in other parts of the application as well.

 I removed the `attr_accessor` method since the new `initialize` method will take care of this for us. If you need the ability to call the data elements outside of the class, then you would still need to have the `attr_accessor` call in place.

To test if the `initialize` method is working, I'm going to create another method in the class that prints these values out:

```
def testing_initializer
  puts @title
  puts @description
  puts @url
end
```

Next, I'll instantiate the class:

```
api = ApiConnector.new("My title", "My cool description", "google.com")
```

Since the `initialize` methods take three parameters, these values have to be passed while creating the class instance or the program will throw an error.

Finally, to test the `initialize` method, I call this:

```
api.testing_initializer
```

If I execute this file on the Terminal, my output will have all the three values printed out:

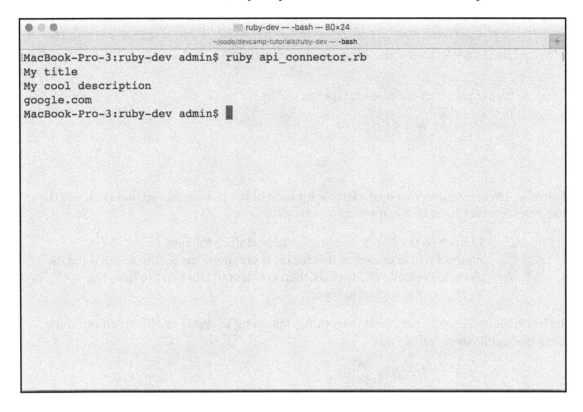

Working with optional values

Now, what happens when we want to make one of these values optional? For example, what if we want to give a default value to the URL? To do that, we can update our `initialize` method with the following syntax:

```
def initialize (title, description, url = "google.com")
```

Now our program will have the same output even if we don't pass the `url` value while creating a new instance of the class. In this case, the output is unchanged when you have the following code:

```
api = ApiConnector.new("My title", "My cool description")
```

This is how you can define optional arguments in an `initialize` method.

Using named arguments

Though this looks simple, passing arguments can get complex in real-world Ruby applications because some methods may take a large number of arguments. In such cases, it becomes difficult to know the order of arguments and what values to assign to them.

To avoid this confusion, I like to utilize named arguments, like this:

```
class ApiConnector
  def initialize (title:, description:, url: "google.com")
    @title = title
    @description = description
    @url = url
  end

  def testing_initializer
    puts @title
    puts @description
    puts @url
  end
end

api = ApiConnector.new(title: "My title", description: "My cool
description")
api.testing_initializer
```

You can enter the arguments without having to look at the order in the `initialize` method. Also, you even change the order of the arguments without causing an error. We can instantiate our class like this:

```
api = ApiConnector.new(description: "My cool description", title: "My
title")
```

This instantiation will not change the behavior of the system. If we weren't using named arguments and if we changed the order of the arguments like this, the instance variables would end up being assigned to the opposite values.

Overriding default values

What happens if we want to override a default value?

We can update our instantiation call like this:

```
api = ApiConnector.new(title: "My title", description: "My cool
description", url: "yahoo.com")
```

This update will override our default value of `google.com`.

The working of OOP inheritance

In this section, we are going to learn about an important object-oriented principle called **inheritance**. Before going into how it is executed in Ruby, let's see why it's important for building applications.

To start with, inheritance means your classes can have a hierarchy. It is best used when different classes have some shared responsibilities, since it would be a poor practice to duplicate code in each class for identical or even similar behavior.

For example, we have been working on our `ApiConnector` class over the last few sections. Let's say we have different API classes for various platforms, but each class shares a number of common data or processes. Instead of duplicating code in each of the API connector classes, we can have one parent class with the shared data and methods. From there, we can create child classes from this parent class. With the way that inheritance works, each of the child classes will have access to the components provided from the parent class.

For example, we have four APIs, namely, `SmsConnector`, `PhoneConnector`, `MailerConnector`, and `XyzConnector`. If we wrote code individually for each of these classes, it would look like this:

```
class SmsConnector
  def initialize(title:, description:, url: 'google.com')
    @title = title
    @description = description
    @url = url
  end

  def send_sms
    puts "Sending SMS message..."
  end
end

class MailerConnector
  def initialize(title:, description:, url: 'google.com')
    @title = title
    @description = description
    @url = url
  end

  def send_mail
```

```
      puts "Sending mail message..."
    end
  end

  class PhoneConnector
    def initialize(title:, description:, url: 'google.com')
      @title = title
      @description = description
      @url = url
    end

    def place_call
      puts "Placing phone call..."
    end
  end

  class XyzConnector
    def initialize(title:, description:, url: 'google.com')
      @title = title
      @description = description
      @url = url
    end

    def does_something_else
      puts "Secret stuff..."
    end
  end
```

As you can see, we are simply repeating the same code across different classes. This is considered a poor programming practice.

Instead, we can make an `ApiConnector` parent class, and each of the other classes can inherit the common functionality from this class:

```
  class ApiConnector
    def initialize(title:, description:, url: 'google.com')
      @title = title
      @description = description
      @url = url
    end
  end

  class SmsConnector < ApiConnector
    def send_sms
      puts "Sending SMS message..."
    end
  end
```

```ruby
class MailerConnector < ApiConnector
  def send_mail
    puts "Sending mail message..."
  end
end

class PhoneConnector < ApiConnector
  def place_call
    puts "Placing phone call..."
  end
end

class XyzConnector < ApiConnector
  def does_something_else
    puts "Secret stuff..."
  end
end
```

By leveraging inheritance, we were able to cut all of the duplicate code throughout our classes.

The syntax for using inheritance is to define the class name followed by the < symbol, followed by the parent class name. For example, our SmsConnector class inherits from the ApiConnector class with the following syntax:

```ruby
class SmsConnector < ApiConnector
```

Each of these child classes now has access to the full set of elements provided in the parent ApiConnector class. We can test this out by adding the attributes to the send_sms method inside of the SmsConnector class, like this:

```ruby
class SmsConnector < ApiConnector
  def send_sms
    puts "Sending SMS message with the #{@title} and #{@description}"
  end
end
```

Now if we create a new instance of SmsConnector with the following parameters, we can call the send_sms method:

```ruby
sms = SmsConnector.new(title: "Hi there!", description: "I'm in a SMS message")
sms.send_sms
```

Running this code will give the following output:

```
Sending SMS message with the Hi there! and I'm in a SMS message
```

A rule of thumb in OOP is to ensure that a class performs a single responsibility. For example, the `ApiConnector` class should not send SMS messages, make phone calls, or send emails since that would be three core responsibilities. Our file is taking a better strategy by creating a child class for each of these functionalities.

For practice, you can create new instances of each class and then call each of the methods present inside the respective classes.

The code to instantiate each of the classes and call the methods is here:

```
sms = SmsConnector.new(title: "Hi there!", description: "I'm in a SMS
message")
mail = MailerConnector.new(title: "Hi there!", description: "I'm in an
email message")
phone = PhoneConnector.new(title: "Hi there!", description: "I'm on a
call")
xyz = XyzConnector.new(title: "Hi there!", description: "Who knows what I'm
in")

sms.send_sms
mail.send_mail
phone.place_call
xyz.does_something_else
```

That's how inheritance works in Ruby. The key to remember about inheritance is that it gives you the ability to clean up your codebase and create inherited classes that share common behavior.

Overview of private versus public methods

This is going to be a fun section, as we are going to talk about sending an SMS message. Also, you will learn about how Ruby works with private and public methods.

Now, I'll go back to the `ApiConnector` class and create a class called `SmsConnector` that inherits from the `ApiConnector` class. In this class, I will create a method called `send_sms`. Inside this method, I'm going to place a code that will run a script that contacts an API that I created; it will look like this:

```
class SmsConnector < ApiConnector
  def send_sms
    `curl -X POST -d "notification[title]=#{@title}" -d
    "notification[url]=http://edutechional-resty.herokuapp.com/posts/1"
    "#{@url}"`
  end
end
```

This method will send a title and link to an API, which will, in turn, send an SMS message. You don't have to worry about the code that will be handling the actual SMS sending, which is part of the beauty of the implementation.

Hopefully, you'll notice that the URL in the method and the URL value we are passing are different. Essentially, the application we're sending the API request to will send the `title` and the URL of the post to my phone. This is cool because we don't have any logic inside our class to send the SMS message. Rather, we are simply processing the data and then connecting to a third-party application that manages SMS communication. This type of application workflow is called **service-based architecture**.

Now we can instantiate the `SmsConnector` class and call the `send_sms` message:

```
sms = SmsConnector.new(title: "Hey there!", url:
"http://edutechional-smsy.herokuapp.com/notifications")
sms.send_sms
```

Running this code will contact the SMS API and send the message.

Private versus public methods

Now, coming back to the types of methods provided by classes, the `send_sms` method is a public method. This means that anyone working on our class can communicate with this method. This may not seem like a big deal if you are working on an application that no one else is working on. However, if you build an API or code library, it's vital that your public methods represent elements of functionality that you actually want other developers to use.

Public methods should rarely, if ever, be altered. This is because other developers may be relying on your public methods to be consistent, and a change to a public method may break components of their programs. Imagine if you developed the Google Maps API and you built a public method called `get_coordinates`, but out of the blue, you altered the method and reversed the order of the coordinates. All of the applications relying on your method will have their maps literally reversed. Obviously, this will upset developers.

So, if you can't change public methods, how can you work on a production application? That's where private methods come in. **Private methods** should never be called by outside services and should only be available within the class that's using them. This means that you can alter the behavior of your private methods (assuming that these changes don't have a domino effect and alter the public methods that they may be called from).

What exactly is a private method? A private method is a method that is only accessed by the class that it is contained in.

 Ruby is so flexible that it allows private methods to be called; however, it is considered a bad programming practice. If a private method really needs to be called by an outside service, either it should be a public method or there is a design problem with the application that's forcing this behavior.

Private method code example

To see what a private method looks like, let's take a look at a real-world Ruby on Rails project that I built:

```
class InventoriesController < ApplicationController
  # Public methods not shown for brevity

  private

    def set_inventory
      @inventory = Inventory.find(params[:id])
    end

    def inventory_params
      params.require(:inventory).permit(:title, :qty, :ticket_id)
    end
end
```

As you can see, in Ruby, we designate private methods using the `private` word above the list of methods. Usually, private methods are placed at the end of the file after all the public methods. Both private methods shown here provide functionality specific to the `InventoriesController` class, and to no other.

Going back to our code example, that is the `ApiConnector` class, let's add a private method like the following:

```
class ApiConnector
  def initialize(title:, url:)
    @title = title
    @url = url
    secret_method
  end

 private

   def secret_method
     puts "A secret message from the parent class"
   end
end

api = ApiConnector.new(title: "My Title", url: "https://devcamp.com")
```

Notice how we're calling this method from the inside of the `initialize` method of the `ApiConnector` class? If we run this code, it will give the following output:

A secret message from the parent class

Now child classes have access to methods in the parent class, right? Well, not always. Let's remove the `secret_method` method from the `initialize` method in `ApiConnector` and try to call it from our `SmsConnector` child class, as shown here:

```
class ApiConnector
  def initialize(title:, url:)
    @title = title
    @url = url
  end

 private

   def secret_method
     puts "A secret message from the parent class"
   end
end
```

```
class SmsConnector < ApiConnector
  def send_sms
    `curl -X POST -d "notification[title]=#{@title}" -d
    "notification[url]=http://edutechional-resty.herokuapp.com/posts/1"
    "#{@url}"`
  end
end

sms = SmsConnector.new(title: "My Title", description: "My Great
Description", url: "http://edutechional-resty.herokuapp.com/notifications")
sms.secret_method
```

The output of the program will be as follows:

```
api_connector.rb:21:in `<main>': private method `secret_method' called for
#<SmsConnector:0x007f99e2823718> (NoMethodError)
```

This is because the SmsConnector class only has access to the public methods from the parent class. The private methods are, by their nature, private. This means that they can only be accessed by the class that they are defined in.

So a good rule of thumb is to create private methods when they should not be used outside the class and public methods when they have to be available throughout the application or by outside services.

 All methods in Ruby are public by default, so you don't have to explicitly declare them as public.

Ruby also has another type of method status called **protected**; however, it is rarely used. We won't worry about it for now.

The working of polymorphism and usage of super

In this guide, we are going to discuss another important concept in OOP called **polymorphism**. Polymorphism occurs when a class that inherits from a parent class overrides the behavior provided by the parent class.

To see a basic example, we'll continue working with our `ApiConnector` class:

```
class ApiConnector
  def initialize(title:, description:, url: 'google.com')
    @title = title
    @description = description
    @url = url
  end

  def api_logger
    puts "API Connector starting..."
  end
end
```

I've added a new method to our class called `api_logger`.

Next, I'll create a class called `PhoneConnector` that inherits from our `ApiConnector` class. After we instantiate the class, it can call the `api_logger` method that we created in the parent class:

```
class PhoneConnector < ApiConnector
end

phone = PhoneConnector.new(title: 'My Title', description: 'Some content')
phone.api_logger
```

If you run this code in the Terminal, you will get the `API Connector Starting...` message.

So how does polymorphism fit in?

Polymorphism occurs when the `PhoneConnector` class overrides the behavior of `api_logger` method, like in the following code:

```
class PhoneConnector < ApiConnector
  def api_logger
    puts "Phone call API connection starting..."
  end
end

phone = PhoneConnector.new(title: 'My Title', description: 'Some content')
phone.api_logger
```

Now, if you run the same code, it prints `Phone call API connection starting....`

This type of polymorphism implementation is quite common in Ruby development and helps developers give some custom behavior to an application.

Next: what happens when we want to combine the behavior from the `api_logger` method of both the `ApiConnector` and `PhoneConnector` classes?

To do that, simply insert the `super` word in the `api_logger` method of the `PhoneConnector` class:

```
class PhoneConnector < ApiConnector
  def api_logger
    super
      puts "Phone call API connection starting..."
  end
end
```

If you run this code, both the messages get displayed:

```
API Connector starting...
Phone call API connection starting...
```

What's making this possible? When Ruby saw the `super` method, it went to the parent class and looked for a method with an identical method and ran that method. Then, it came back to the method in the child class and finished running the rest of the code in the method.

That's how polymorphism and super work in Ruby.

Dead simple OOP

Through my years of teaching, one of the most common questions I get from developers is how to best understand OOP. OOP development can seem a bit intimidating if you've never used it before. So I wanted to take a step back and give a high-level perspective of how it can be used to build applications.

My history with OOP

When I started programming over a decade ago, I learned how to build applications procedurally with languages such as C and PHP. If you're not familiar with procedural code, it simply means that you build programs in sequential order and call methods when you want shared behavior between pages in the application. For example, if I had an invoicing application, I'd have a page for creating a new invoice, another page for showing the invoice, and so on. And each page would have scripts that would call methods such as ones connecting it to the database or rendering a date in a specific format.

How does OOP work?

Now that you have a high-level view of how procedural programming works, how does OOP work? I like to think of OOP as a way of modeling a program, where all of the functionality is abstracted so it can be shared throughout the application. Let's take a look at a real-world case study.

Imagine that you're building an application that allows users to create accounts and you also need to have the ability to make some people administrators. In OOP, you have a `User` class, which has the following methods:

- Register
- Sign in
- Encrypt password

Now, we have the issue that you have two types of users—regular users and site administrators. For the most part, both user types are pretty similar the only differences will be things such as editing pages and admin type tasks. In procedural programming, you'd need to create two different types of users, which would lead to having quite a bit of duplicate code. However, in OOP, you can simply create a `User` class, and then create the `RegularUser` and `AdminUser` classes that inherit from the parent `User` class.

When child classes inherit from the parent class they get access to all of the methods and functionality of the parent class, and then you as a developer can give them custom behavior. So, for our case study, the `AdminUser` class would contain methods unique to it that the `RegularUser` class wouldn't have, which would give it the administrator functionality.

Do you see how that works?

OOP, at a high level, is all about being able to structure code in a way where its functionality can be inherited and behavior modified in any way that the developer sees fit. If done properly, OOP can lead to very elegantly written programs that have minimal code duplication.

I hope you now have a better idea of how OOP works.

SOLID OOP development – the simple responsibility principle

In this section focusing on the SOLID development pattern and how it applies to OOP, we will walk through the single responsibility principle. While the concept of single responsibility has been around for a while, it was popularized in 2003 by Uncle Bob.

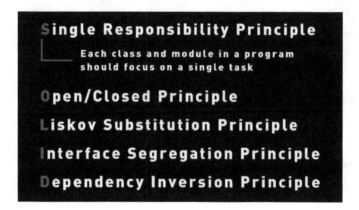

The single responsibility principle

What exactly is the **Single Responsibility Principle (SRP)**? The term is pretty self descriptive. Essentially, it means that each class and module in a program should focus on a single task.

The SRP in the real world

Before we go into a code example, let's look at the real-world case study of a vacuum cleaner. A vacuum cleaner can perform a number of tasks such as cleaning floors and upholstery. Some of the more upscale vacuums can even work like a blower. However, notice how, at its core, a vacuum has an engine that utilizes air to perform the task of cleaning?

It wouldn't make sense for a vacuum cleaner to also wash windows. If you introduced this type of feature to the vacuum it may work for a while, but would most likely cause increased maintenance costs when it would inevitably break down.

An SRP example

Now that you have an idea of how the SRP works in the real world, let's dive into a code example.

The class that knew too much

Here we have an `Invoice` class that seems to be relatively straightforward:

- It prints out details about the invoice
- It calculates sales tax
- It emails the invoice with its details

Following is the implementation of the `Invoice` class:

```
class Invoice
  def initialize(customer:, state:, total:)
    @customer = customer
    @state = state
    @total = total
  end

  def details
    "Customer: #{@customer}, Total: #{@total}"
  end

  def sales_tax
    case @state
    when 'AZ' then 5.5
    when 'TX' then 3.2
    when 'CA' then 8.7
    end
  end

  def email_invoice
    puts "Emailing invoice..."
    puts details
  end
end

invoice = Invoice.new(customer: "Google", state: "AZ", total: 100)
puts invoice.sales_tax
invoice.email_invoice
```

When we run this code, everything works fine and prints out these values:

```
5.5
Emailing invoice...
Customer: Google, Total: 100
```

This may seem fine at first; however, this code is breaking the SRP in a number of ways.

Rule of thumb – no ands allowed

When it comes to following the SOLID design pattern, a good rule of thumb is that if your description of a class has the word *and* in it, then it may need to be refactored. For example, let's describe this class:

The Invoice class prints out invoice details *and* calculates sales tax *and* emails the invoice.

Whenever I'm performing a refactor, I like to treat the behavior between the *ands* as their own class.

A mailer class

Here we have created a new class called `Mailer` that has a single method that will send out an email. The `email` method takes an argument where we can pass the invoice details to it:

```ruby
class Invoice
  def initialize(customer:, state:, total:)
    @customer = customer
    @state = state
    @total = total
  end

  def details
    "Customer: #{@customer}, Total: #{@total}"
  end

  def sales_tax
    case @state
    when 'AZ' then 5.5
    when 'TX' then 3.2
    when 'CA' then 8.7
    end
  end
end

class Mailer
  def self.email(content)
    puts "Emailing..."
    puts content
  end
end

invoice = Invoice.new(customer: "Google", state: "AZ", total: 100)
puts invoice.sales_tax
Mailer.email(invoice.details)
```

If we run this code, we'll see this is working properly:

```
5.5
Emailing invoice...
Customer: Google, Total: 100
```

The sales tax class

Next is our sales tax feature. This component definitely shouldn't be included in the Invoice class since it doesn't take much imagination to realize that this feature may be required by other parts of an application outside of the invoice:

```ruby
class Invoice
  def initialize(customer:, state:, total:)
    @customer = customer
    @total = total
  end

  def details
    "Customer: #{@customer}, Total: #{@total}"
  end
end

class SalesTax
  def initialize(state:)
    @state = state
  end

  def sales_tax
    case @state
    when 'AZ' then 5.5
    when 'TX' then 3.2
    when 'CA' then 8.7
    end
  end
end

class Mailer
  def self.email(content)
    puts "Emailing..."
    puts content
  end
end

invoice = Invoice.new(customer: "Google", state: "AZ", total: 100)
tax = SalesTax.new(state: 'CA')
puts tax.sales_tax
```

```
Mailer.email(invoice.details)
```

Here, we created a `SalesTax` class that takes in the state we want to generate the sales tax for. Running this code will show that our program is still working perfectly:

```
8.7
Emailing...
Customer: Google, Total: 100
```

Now our `Invoice` class is following the SRP. Can you see how the invoice is no longer in charge of generating sales tax or emailing customers?

Why the SRP is important

Why is this type of OOP design pattern important? Our initial `Invoice` code worked fine, so why would we have to change it? Let's imagine that this program was used by a real-world accounting division. What if a user wanted to see what the tax rate would be for a specific state? It wouldn't make sense for the system to require the user to create an invoice to calculate that value.

By refactoring the program in the way we did in this guide, our `SalesTax` class could be used independently or by any other classes that may need the feature. In the computer science world, this concept is called **coupling**. In our initial code example, the sales tax component was highly coupled to the `Invoice` class. This means that it would be messy to work with the tax rate generator without having to also work with the `Invoice` class.

Our refactor fixed this issue and now we can say that the tax feature has low coupling. This means that users can access the tax rate component without having to work with other classes.

SOLID OOP development – the open/closed principle guide and example

Continuing on our discussion of SOLID development principles, in this guide I'll walk you through the **open/closed principle**:

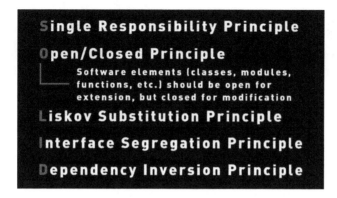

For some reason or another, developers seem to struggle understanding this SOLID element more than some of the others. With this in mind, I'll give a dead simple explanation of how the open/closed principle works, followed by a Ruby code example.

I think that once you see how powerful this concept is, you'll fall in love with it because, at it's core, it allows you to scale your code without having to worry about wasting time on legacy classes.

The open/closed principle definition

A dead simple explanation of the open/closed principle is this:

Software elements (classes, modules, functions, and so on) should be open for extension, but closed for modification.

Essentially, this means that you should build your classes in a way that you can extend them via child classes. Once you've created the parent class, it no longer needs to be changed.

The original concept was credited to Bertrand Meyer when he coined the term back in 1988 in his book, *Object-Oriented Software Construction, Prentice Hall.*

A surprisingly challenging task

If you've never attempted this design pattern, the concept may seem straightforward. However, I think you'll find this is a skill that takes practice and repetition (much like any other advanced development task).

The open/closed principle example

To understand how the open/closed principle works, let's look at a practical example.

The naive approach

I created an `OrderReport` class that contains some attributes such as `customer` and `total`. In addition to these attributes, the class also contains a couple of methods, as shown here:

- An `invoice` method that prints out the details associated with an order
- A `bill_of_lading` method that prints out the order report for shipping purposes

```ruby
class OrderReport
  def initialize(customer:, total:)
    @customer = customer
    @total = total
  end

  def invoice
    puts "Invoice"
    puts @customer
    puts @total
  end

  def bill_of_lading
    puts "BOL"
    puts @customer
    puts "Shipping Label..."
  end
end

order = OrderReport.new(customer: "Google", total: 100)
order.invoice
order.bill_of_lading
```

If you run this program, you'll see that it works perfectly fine and prints out the values for each method:

```
Invoice
Google
100
BOL
Google
Shipping Label...
```

I don't like change!

However, this `OrderReport` class has a nasty secret—it doesn't like change. Let's imagine that we're asked to update the `bill_of_lading` method to also print out the customer address:

```ruby
class OrderReport
  def initialize(customer:, total:, address:)
    @customer = customer
    @total = total
    @address = address
  end

  def invoice
    puts "Invoice"
    puts @customer
    puts @total
  end

  def bill_of_lading
    puts "BOL"
    puts @customer
    puts "Shipping Label..."
    puts @address
  end
end

order = OrderReport.new(customer: "Google",
                        total: 100,
                        address: "123 Any Street")
order.invoice
order.bill_of_lading
```

This may not seem like a major change; however, in order to accommodate the request, we had to make four changes.

One of the changes is even requiring us to pass an address to the class as a required argument. This means that even when all we need is an invoice (that doesn't care about the customer address), we have to include the additional element.

Also of note is that this was a very small change. Imagine what would happen if we needed to build a feature such as including a QR code or something complex like that?

It not only lacks scalability, it's also breaking the open/closed principle. A well-written class should not have to be rewritten in order to integrate a new feature such as having an address.

A better way

Thankfully, we can clean up this entire class and follow the open/closed principle by leveraging object-oriented inheritance:

```ruby
class OrderReport
  def initialize(customer:, total:)
    @customer = customer
    @total = total
  end
end

class Invoice < OrderReport
  def print_out
    puts "Invoice"
    puts @customer
    puts @total
  end
end

class BillOfLading < OrderReport
  def initialize(address:, **args)
    super(**args)
    @address = address
  end

  def print_out
    puts "BOL"
    puts @customer
    puts "Shipping Label..."
    puts @address
  end
end

invoice = Invoice.new(customer: "Google",
                      total: 100)

bill_of_lading = BillOfLading.new(customer: "Yahoo",
                                  total: 200,
                                  address: "123 Any Street")

invoice.print_out
bill_of_lading.print_out
```

In this code, I pulled out the invoice and bill of lading components into their own classes that inherit from the `OrderReport` class.

This refactor has a number of benefits:

- It follows the open/closed principle because now when we have to build new features for invoices or bills of lading, we don't have to touch the `OrderReport` class. Therefore, we can say that the parent class is closed.
- Additionally, since we split up the two components, whenever we create an invoice we don't have to pass in an unnecessary address element. This removes code that's not needed and that could lead to confusion later on down the road.
- Lastly, our program not only follows the open/closed principle but now our classes also follow the SRP. Do you notice how each class has a specific focus (also known as, a single responsibility)?

If you run this code, you'll see that it still has the same behavior as before, but now our code is much more scalable and dare I say, SOLID?

SOLID OOP development – the Liskov substitution principle

Continuing on our discussion of SOLID OOP development principles, in this guide, we'll walk through the **Liskov Substitution Principle (LSP)**:

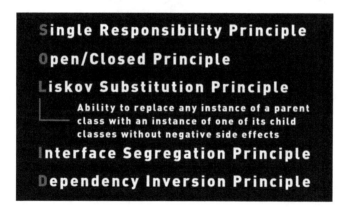

When it comes to object-oriented development, the LSP can be slightly confusing to Ruby developers. Part of the confusion comes from the fact that this principle has more of an effect with statically typed languages, such as Java. However, it's still an important concept to understand, so stay tuned and I'll walk you through a practical example of how this applies to all OOP languages.

The LSP definition

To be 100 percent transparent, I struggled through researching this topic. However, what helped me understand it was this:

- Talking it through with a software engineer that I respect (Chase Baker)
- Breaking down the definition into very small pieces

With that in mind, let's walk through a dead simple definition of the concept. The LSP states this:

A program should have the ability to replace any instance of a parent class with an instance of one of its child classes without negative side effects.

Breaking down the LSP

If that's about as clear as mud, don't worry; this principle isn't for the faint of heart. It helped me tremendously to break the definition apart, so let's give that a shot.

We'll start with the fact that we know we're going to be working with replacing instances of classes.

Next we know that we're going to be working with parent and child classes. This tells me that the principle revolves around object-oriented inheritance.

Lastly, it sounds like programs have to be able to allow for child class instances to seamlessly replace parent classes. This tells me that we need to focus on the messages that are sent along with ensuring that our parent and child classes can't have requirements that would cause conflicts.

Still confused? That's fine, this concept took me longer to understand than all of the other SOLID principles combined. So you're in good company.

The LSP example

The following is an example for the LSP:

```
require 'date'

class User
  attr_accessor :settings, :email
```

```
    def initialize(email:)
      @email = email
    end
  end

  class AdminUser < User
  end

  user = User.new(email: "user@test.com")
  user.settings = {
    level: "Low Security",
    status: "Live",
    signed_in: Date.today
  }

  admin = AdminUser.new(email: "admin@test.com")
  admin.settings = ["Editor", "VIP", Date.today]

  puts user.settings
  puts admin.settings
```

For our code walk-through, I created a basic `User` class in Ruby. Additionally, I built an `AdminUser` class that inherits from the parent `User` class. The classes have attributes for settings and an email.

In our case study, we decided to make an interesting decision to use the hash data type for our settings in the `User` class. However, we're using the array data type for our `AdminUser` class settings. This seems like an innocuous issue because when we run this program, both classes seem to be working fine:.

```
{:level=>"Low Security", :status=>"Live", :signed_in=>#<Date: 2016-09-23
((2457655j,0s,0n),+0s,2299161j)>}
Editor
VIP
2016-09-23
```

The problem

Our problem may not be evident quite yet. However, watch what happens when we need to build a new feature:

```
require 'date'

class User
  attr_accessor :settings, :email
```

```ruby
  def initialize(email:)
    @email = email
  end
end

class AdminUser < User
end

user = User.new(email: "user@test.com")
user.settings = {
  level: "Low Security",
  status: "Live",
  signed_in: Date.today
}

admin = AdminUser.new(email: "admin@test.com")
admin.settings = ["Editor", "VIP", Date.today]

@user_database = [user, admin]

def signed_in_today?
  @user_database.each do |user|
    if user.settings[:signed_in] == Date.today
    puts "#{user.email} signed in today"
    end
  end
end

signed_in_today?
```

Our new feature is a script called `signed_in_today?` that will run each day and generate a report that lists out which users logged in that day. It combines both regular and admin users into an instance variable called `@user_database`. From there it loops over the settings for all of the users to see if the user signed in that day or not.

This is a pretty common feature, but let's see what happens when we run this code:

```
user@test.com signed in today
solid.rb:28:in `[]': no implicit conversion of Symbol into Integer
(TypeError)
      from solid.rb:28:in `block in signed_in_today?'
      from solid.rb:27:in `each'
      from solid.rb:27:in `signed_in_today?'
      from solid.rb:34:in `<main>'
```

Our script works perfectly fine for our user that was created straight from the `User` class. However, it breaks when it comes to our `admin` user and gives the `no implicit conversion of Symbol into Integer (TypeError)` error.

The bug with this program is relatively straightforward. Our `signed_in_today?` method is looking for settings that are stored as a hash data type. However, when it encounters the `AdminUser` settings, which are stored with the array data type, it throws an error.

The LSP violation

So does this example qualify as a LSP violation? Let's look at the definition again:

A program should have the ability to replace any instance of a parent class with an instance of one of its child classes without negative side effects.

In our example, we attempted to substitute an instance of a child class, our `AdminUser` class, for its parent class. By performing this action, it broke the program, which I think qualifies as a negative side effect.

The fix

Now let's see what we need to do to fix this. You may think it's as easy as changing the admin `settings` call so that we pass it a hash, like this:

```
admin = AdminUser .new(email: "admin@test.com" )
admin.settings = {
  level: "Editor" ,
  status: "VIP" ,
  signed_in: Date .today
}
```

Yes, technically, that would work for this one instance. However, this doesn't fix the core problem, and the same bug will continue to happen if a developer forgets that `settings` need to be a hash. So what's a better solution? Personally, I'd attack the root issue and force the program to only have one option when it comes to saving settings:

```
require 'date'
require 'ostruct'

class User
  attr_accessor :settings, :email
```

```ruby
    def initialize(email:)
      @email = email
    end

    def set_settings(level:, status:, signed_in:)
      @settings = OpenStruct.new(
                    level: level,
                    status: status,
                    signed_in: signed_in
                  )
    end

    def get_settings
      @settings
    end
  end

  class AdminUser < User
  end

  user = User.new(email: "user@test.com")
  user.settings = {
    level: "Low Security",
    status: "Live",
    signed_in: Date.today
  }

  admin = AdminUser.new(email: "admin@test.com")
  admin.settings = {
    level: "Editor",
    status: "VIP",
    signed_in: Date.today
  }

  @user_database = [user, admin]

  def signed_in_today?
    @user_database.each do |user|
      if user.settings[:signed_in] == Date.today
        puts "#{user.email} signed in today"
      end
    end
  end

  signed_in_today?
```

In this code, I'm importing the Ruby `OpenStruct` library. Next, I remove `settings` as an attribute of the class and, instead, I create a method called `set_settings` that can be called, and save the setting into the `OpenStruct` data type. Then `settings` can be called from anywhere in the application for the `User` class and any child classes it may have, and we can trust the behavior that it will generate.

Now our `AdminUser` class instances can replace any instances of the `User` class and the program will still work properly.

SOLID OOP development – the interface segregation principle

As we make our way through the SOLID development journey, it's time we turned to the I in SOLID, which represents the **Interface Segregation Principle (ISP)**:

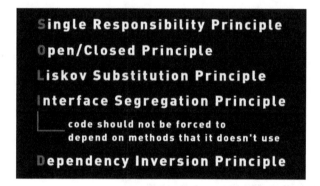

The ISP definition

As with several of the other SOLID design concepts, this represents a scary name for an important topic. A dead simple definition of the ISP is that code should not be forced to depend on methods that it doesn't use.

If this is a bit fuzzy, don't worry, I'm going to walk you through a code example that clears it up.

Believe it or not, this is one of the easier SOLID concepts to understand and work with.

The ISP code example

Let's start by taking a look at a program that manages a blog:

```ruby
class Blog
  def edit_post
    puts "Post edited"
  end

  def delete_post
    puts "Post removed"
  end

  def create_post
    puts "Post created"
  end
end

blog = Blog.new
blog.edit_post
blog.delete_post
blog.create_post
```

Obviously, this program simply prints out some values in each method. If we run the program, you'll see that this code works properly:

```
Post edited
Post removed
Post created
```

Introducing the moderator

Now what happens if we want to create a `Moderator` class? On a side note—let's ignore the fact that a `Moderator` class should never be connected or inherited from a `Blog` class since a moderator isn't a type of blog. However, in preparing for this guide, I walked through a number of examples and, this case study, illustrated the ISP the best.

Our `Moderator` class is very specialized. Moderators should only be able to edit a post. However, this poses a problem if we try to use code like this:

```ruby
class Blog
  def edit_post
    puts "Post edited"
  end
```

```
  def delete_post
    puts "Post removed"
  end

  def create_post
    puts "Post created"
  end
end

  class Moderator < Blog
  end

  moderator = Moderator.new
  moderator.edit_post
  moderator.delete_post
  moderator.create_post
```

The problem with this `Moderator` class is that it not only can edit posts but also delete posts. For practical reasons, this is bad. However, it is also breaking the ISP because we intertwined our `Blog` class with our `Moderator` class. Even though `Moderator` may not directly depend on all of the `Blog` methods, it's still coupled with them since they can be called from instances of the class.

A better way

Thankfully, Ruby offers us a better way of giving us the behavior that we need. By leveraging the `Forwardable` module we can limit the scope of what our `Moderator` class can access:

```
require 'forwardable'

class Blog
  def edit_post
    puts "Post edited"
  end

  def delete_post
    puts "Post removed"
  end

  def create_post
    puts "Post created"
  end
end
```

```
class Moderator
  extend Forwardable
  def_delegators :@blog, :edit_post

  def initialize(blog)
    @blog = blog
  end
end

moderator = Moderator.new(Blog.new)
moderator.edit_post
moderator.delete_post
```

This code starts by importing the `Forwardable` module in both the file and inside the `Moderator` class. Next we update the `Moderator` class so it no longer inherits from `Blog`. With those components cleaned up, we can leverage the `Forwardable` module's `def_delegators` method to list what we want the `Moderator` class to have access to.

In this case, we want the `Moderator` class to have access to the `Blog` class and the `edit_post` method inside of `Blog`. Notice how this is different than having `Moderator` inherit from `Blog`? Instead of giving access to the full class definition, we're able to pick and choose what elements `Moderator` should be able to work with.

Next, we'll set up an `initialize` method that takes a `blog` as an argument. This is how we're letting Ruby know that our `Moderator` class needs to be passed to the `Blog` class as an argument.

Lastly, we can instantiate a new `Moderator` and pass in a new `Blog` instance as an argument.

The result

After running this code, you'll see that our moderator can edit posts successfully:

```
Post edited

solid.rb:28:in `<main>': undefined method `delete_post' for
#<Moderator:0x007f7f5189a9e0 @blog=#<Blog:0x007f7f5189aa08>>
(NoMethodError)
```

However, when it tries to delete a post it gets an error since we didn't give it access to that method.

A caveat

Before ending this guide, I want to make one point of clarification. The walk through I just went through is specific to how you can work with the ISP in the Ruby language. However, since Ruby is a dynamic language it doesn't require developers to declare class and method types. The ISP has a number of other requirements for statically typed languages such as Java or C++. So keep that in mind if you work with those types of languages.

Ruby does quite a bit of the hard work for us when it comes to object-oriented development; however, this is still an important concept to understand, and, as a bonus you were able to learn about the `Forwardable` module!

SOLID OOP development – the dependency inversion principle

In this guide, we'll walk through the final element of the SOLID development pattern, the **Dependency Inversion Principle (DIP)**.

If you have had a difficult time understanding some of the other SOLID guides, you'll be happy to know that this principle is probably the most straightforward.

The DIP in the real world

The reason why I think that the DIP is easy to understand is that it relates to a real-world pattern. Before we jump into the code, we'll look at how a large company is structured.

Let's imagine that you're the CEO of Coca-Cola. As the CEO of a multibillion dollar company, you will have a number of responsibilities. Some of these tasks might be as follows:

- Managing shareholders
- Making strategic acquisitions
- Deciding which markets to enter
- Also, a number of other high-level decisions

Now let's look at what you wouldn't do as the CEO of Coca-Cola:

- Drive a truck and make product deliveries
- Pick SEO keywords for the corporate website
- Work on tax rate calculations for the accounting system

You get the idea.

As a CEO, it would be your job to manage the organization and delegate responsibilities to the executives that report to you. If you spent your time with low-level work such as making deliveries to 7-11 customers you wouldn't be able to properly manage the company.

The DIP definition

In a nutshell, this is how the DIP works.

The definition for the DIP is this:

High level objects should not depend on low-level implementations.

In the same way that the Coca-Cola CEO shouldn't double as a truck driver, high-level code shouldn't perform low-level duties.

The DIP code example

For our code example we're going to take a look at how the Ruby on Rails framework uses the `ActiveRecord` module:

```
require "active_support"
require "active_support/rails"
require "active_model"
require "arel"

require "active_record/version"
require "active_record/attribute_set"

moduleActiveRecord
  extend ActiveSupport::Autoload

  autoload:Attribute
  autoload:Base
  autoload:Callbacks
  autoload:Core
  autoload:ConnectionHandling
  autoload:CounterCache
  autoload:DynamicMatchers
  autoload:Enum
  autoload:InternalMetadata
  autoload:Explain
  autoload:Inheritance
  autoload:Integration
  autoload:LegacyYamlAdapter
  autoload:Migration
  autoload:Migrator, "active_record/migration"
  autoload:ModelSchema
  autoload:NestedAttributes
  autoload:NoTouching
  autoload:TouchLater
  # Tons of other method calls
```

The `ActiveRecord` class is a powerful module that allows applications to interface with the database.

What do you think would have happened if the developers who built the Rails framework attempted to place specific implementation details in the framework? For example, what if they added a database query for users? It would essentially render the framework useless because it would only work if developers built out a `User` class that matched the vision of the Rails developers.

Thankfully, the Rails development team chose to follow the DIP. If you analyze the `ActiveRecord` module source code, you'll see that the code is simply concerned with high-level functionality. This means that `ActiveRecord` will let you do the following things:

- Search for records in a database
- Allow you to call data validations
- Utilize callbacks for automated behavior
- Utilize callbacks for additional high-level tools
- Inherit classes to manage implementation

So what does the other side of the equation look like? If the parent class, in this case `ActiveRecord`, manages the high-level behavior, let's take a look at a child class:

```ruby
class User < ActiveRecord::Base
  has_many :posts
  has_many :audit_logs

  has_many :hands_associations, class_name: 'Hand'
  has_many :hands, through: :hands_associations
  # Include default devise modules. Others available are:
  # :confirmable, :lockable, :timeoutable and :omniauthable
   devise :database_authenticatable, :registerable,
      :recoverable, :rememberable, :trackable, :validatable

  validates_presence_of :first_name, :last_name, :phone, :ssn, :company

  PHONE_REGEX = /\A[0-9]*\Z/

  validates_format_of :phone, with: PHONE_REGEX

  validates :phone, length: { is: 10 }
  validates :ssn, length: { is: 4 }
  validates_numericality_of :ssn

  def full_name
    last_name.upcase + ", " + first_name.upcase
  end
end
```

Here is a class called `User` that inherits from `ActiveRecord::Base`. This class contains the following implementation details:

- Listing out specific attributes
- Mapping the `User` class to other models in the application
- Defining data validations for attributes that the `User` class manages

Recap

So, let's review our code example:

- The `ActiveRecord` module is like the application's CEO. It manages high-level functionality with zero implementation details. This allows the module to be used for any type of application and for all models inside an application.
- While the `User` class is like one of the application's workers, it focuses on the low-level implementation details. It listens to the `ActiveRecord` parent class and follows the guidelines laid out, much like how an employee listens to a CEO's instructions.

Overall, the DIP is a powerful design pattern that allows you to build scalable code that can be leveraged throughout an application.

Summary

This chapter covered a lot of important concepts. This chapter's primary goal was to examine how OOP can be utilized to limit duplicate code and share core functionality between subclasses. Initially, we walked through a real-world example of OOP and saw how to implement setters and getters in Ruby classes. You looked at the concept of instantiation and learned the `initialize` method in Ruby, including its syntax, when it can be helpful to use, and various options you can pass to it in order to perform tasks such as setting default values.

We saw one of the important building blocks of OOP development—inheritance. The key to remember about inheritance is that it gives you the ability to clean up your codebase and create inherited classes that share common behavior. We reviewed the differences between private and public methods in Ruby classes. We analyzed how to categorize methods and we took a high-level view of method visibility.

Another important concept of OOP that we walked through was the concept of polymorphism, which is simply a tool in your OOP arsenal that allows you to alter the behavior of parent methods in a subclass.

Lastly, we looked at the SOLID (SRP, open/closed, LSP, ISP, and DIP) design principles.

In the next chapter, we'll analyze how to work with the Ruby filesystem.

10
Working with the Filesystem in Ruby

In this chapter, we'll explore various ways to work with files in Ruby, including the ability to create, open, edit, and delete files using built-in methods and classes. After you have completed this chapter, you will be able to do the following:

- Demonstrate how to work with the `File` class in order to generate, read, edit, append, and delete files in Ruby
- Explain how file permissions work with the Ruby `File` class methods

Creating a file

In this section, we will learn how to work with files in Ruby, including how to create, edit, and append to a file. This information can be particularly helpful when you want to store content in data in a file, so that you don't have to rely on a database connection every time. It's good to have some practical knowledge of this.

Ruby File class

First off, we are going to see how to create a file:

```
File.open("files-lessons/teams.txt" , 'w+')  { |f| f.write("Twins, Astros,
Mets, Yankees") }
```

In this code, I'm calling a core Ruby class called File and I'm passing two values as the parameters to its open method. The first parameter is the path where I want my text file to be located and the second is the options that I want to do with the file. In this case, w+ stands for reading and writing.

Other options you can pass as the second option

Following is the list of the options you can pass as the second option:

- r: This stands for reading
- a: This stands for appending to a file
- w: This stands for just writing to a file
- w+: This stands for reading and writing to a file
- a+: This stands for opening a file for reading and appending
- r+: This stands for opening a file for updating, and it includes both reading and writing

Going back to the code, the f variable is the block variable, and we are asking it to write all the values that are present inside the double quotes by passing the write method to it.

If you run this code, it will create a text file called teams.txt and add the names of the four teams inside it.

To run it, go to the Terminal and type the following command (or run it from wherever you have saved it on your system):

```
ruby files-lessons/creating_a_file.rb
```

Now, if you go back to the files-lessons folder, you will see a new file called teams.txt, and if you open it, you can find Twins, Astros, Mets, Yankees in it.

There is also another way to accomplish this functionality for your future reference:

```
file_to_save = File.new("files-lessons/otherteams.txt" , 'w+')
file_to_save.puts("A's, Diamondbacks, Mariners, Marlins")
file_to_save.close
```

Now, if you run this code, you can see the otherteams.txt file, which has the A's, Diamondbacks, Mariners, Marlins content.

Reading files into a program using the File class

Ruby does some cool things when it comes to reading from a file, and we will see that in this guide.

In the previous guide, we created a file containing the names of baseball teams. You can ask Ruby to read the contents of this file with the following code line:

```
teams = File.read("files-lessons/teams.txt")
```

If you print the `teams` variable, your output should be the names of all the teams stored in that file.

Now, let's say we want to do something with the contents of a file. First, we have to separate the values and put them in an array. The code for this task is as follows:

```
p teams.split
```

The `split` method will look at the string of the text and separate each element that is separated by a space.

If you execute it, you'll see that the values turned into an array:

```
["Twins,", "Astros,", "Mets,", "Yankees"]
```

If you don't like the , symbol after every element in the array, you can remove that too by adding an argument to the `split` method:

```
p teams.split(',')
```

The `split` function takes a delimiter as its argument. So, if you run it now, the output should be as follows:

```
["Twins", " Astros", " Mets", " Yankees"]
```

So, that's how you can convert the values in a file into an array.

Next, let's assume we have teams spread across multiple files, and we want to get all of them into the same array. To do this, enter this:

```
teams_one = File.read("files-lessons/teams.txt")
teams_two = File.read("files-lessons/other_teams.txt")

p teams_one.split(',') + teams_two.split(',')
```

If you run this code, this is how your output should be:

```
["Twins", " Astros", " Mets", " Yankees", "A's", " Diamondbacks", "
Mariners", " Marlins"]
```

We can now do whatever we want with this combined array. For example, you can turn it all into uppercase:

```
teams_one = File.read("files-lessons/teams.txt")
teams_two = File.read("files-lessons/otherteams.txt")

teams_master = teams_one.split(',') + teams_two.split(',')

teams_master.each { |team| p team.upcase }
```

If you run this code, your output should have all the teams printed in uppercase:

```
"TWINS"
"ASTROS"
"METS"
"YANKEES"
"A'S"
"DIAMONDBACKS"
"MARINERS"
"MARLINS"
```

So that's how you can not only read files in Ruby but also practically work with the data contained in them.

Deleting a file

Now that we know how to create a file and read from it, let's learn how to delete a file. It can be done with a single line of code, like this:

```
File.delete("files-lessons/teams.txt")
```

Execute this code, and go back to the directory of your file. The file has been removed.

That's all there is to deleting a file. However, you should be careful while using this command as you don't want to accidentally delete a file. Remember, Ruby offers no warning whatsoever before deleting, so make sure you use it carefully.

Appending a file

In this section, you will learn something that is very practical: how to append information to the end of a file. We'll take the case study of creating a log file that we add data to at various intervals. This is a common feature that you'll need to build in a real-world Ruby project, so this is an important skill to learn.

Building a log file

The following is a simple example code for building a log file:

```
do
  sleep 1
  puts "Record saved..."
  File.open("files-lessons/server_logs.txt", "a") {|f|
  f.puts"Server started at: #{Time.new}"}
end
```

In this code, we create or open a file called `server_logs.txt` in the append mode. In this file, we append the time when our server started. We run it through a loop with `f` being the block variable. We do it ten times with a one second break between each iteration.

 Whenever you want to mimic a process, or in this case, ensure that each iteration occurs at a different time, it's common to leverage the `sleep` method, which takes the number of seconds the process should pause as the argument.

When you run this file, your output should have the `Record saved...` message written ten times:

```
Record saved...
Record saved...
Record saved...
Record saved...
Record saved...
Record saved...
```

```
Record saved...
Record saved...
Record saved...
Record saved...
```

Now, if you open the file called `server_logs.txt`, you get to see the timestamp, with a one second break:

```
Server started at: 2016-09-05 17:49:18 -0500
Server started at: 2016-09-05 17:49:19 -0500
Server started at: 2016-09-05 17:49:20 -0500
Server started at: 2016-09-05 17:49:21 -0500
Server started at: 2016-09-05 17:49:22 -0500
Server started at: 2016-09-05 17:49:23 -0500
Server started at: 2016-09-05 17:49:24 -0500
Server started at: 2016-09-05 17:49:25 -0500
Server started at: 2016-09-05 17:49:26 -0500
Server started at: 2016-09-05 17:49:27 -0500
```

Let's run this file one more time to see if values are getting appended to our file. If you open the `server_logs.txt` file, you should see 20 records because we've run the code twice.

So, this is a component that you can build in a real-life application.

Summary

In this chapter, we walked through the basic components that comprise the Ruby `File` class and also reviewed the list of options that you can use when creating or adding to files. We analyzed how you can read the contents of files into Ruby programs by utilizing the `read` method. We also examined how to iterate over each line in a file and perform operations on each line. We learned how to delete files in Ruby. However, you should be careful while using this command as you don't want to accidentally delete a file. Remember, Ruby offers no warning whatsoever before deleting, so make sure you use it carefully. This chapter also walked you through the commands for appending content to the end of a file. Appending content to the end of a file is a great way of adding persistence to a Ruby program, without having to integrate a full database such as PostgreSQL or MySQL. Additionally, we walked through a practical implementation for building a log file and dynamically adding content to the end of a file.

In the next chapter, we'll analyze how to handle errors in Ruby.

11
Error Handling in Ruby

Many new developers are intimidated when they come across errors and exceptions in a program. However, errors are Ruby's way of telling you how you can improve or alter your program to work properly. In this chapter, you'll learn how to work with errors in Ruby, including learning how to build practical tools such as an error logging program. Additionally, you'll be able to do the following:

- Categorize exceptions in a Ruby program
- Demonstrate how to properly implement an error management system

Error handling tutorial

In this guide, we will discuss error handling in Ruby. Error handling is important to know when your application has run into a bug, so that you know how to fix it accordingly.

To see how it works, let's start with creating a line of code that will generate an error:

```
puts 8/0
```

If you execute it, your application will throw an error:

```
error_handling.rb:1:in `/': divided by 0 (ZeroDivisionError)
    from error_handling.rb:1:in `<main>'
```

This code is attempting to divide by zero (which isn't possible), so it's running into `ZeroDivisionError`. To handle this error in a more elegant way, the syntax is as follows:

```
begin
  puts 8/0
rescue
  puts "Rescued the error"
end
```

If you run this code, the program will print out `Rescued the error`.

Though the error is more elegant, it does not really fix the bug. In fact, this implementation is a poor choice when it comes to managing errors. A better way would be to know what the error is, so you can make the right fix.

I hope this gives you an idea of a basic way to handle errors. In the following sections, we'll walk through the proper techniques for implementing error handling in Ruby programs that follow best practices.

Error handling – the best practices

Though the previous guide walked through basic error handling that works in practice, there is always room for improvement. In this guide, you are going to learn better error handling techniques in Ruby.

Sometimes, we may not want to rescue every error because we may actually be doing something wrong, such as entering bad data into the database. In such cases, we are better off rescuing only specific errors. For example, let's say you want 8/0 to proceed, but only want it to be logged, so the system knows something like this happened.

To catch the error properly let's include our `begin` and `rescue` blocks, but this time, specify the error that needs to be rescued:

```
begin
  puts 8/0
rescue ZeroDivisionError => e
  puts "Error occurred: #{e}"
end
```

In this code, we are moving the description associated with `ZeroDivisionError` to the `e` variable and printing it out like a normal variable.

If you execute this code, the output will be `Error occurred: divided by 0`.

This format can be particularly useful when printing error messages to a log file, as it would give a better explanation of what went wrong that we can reference later on when performing debugging.

Let's try something else now. Change the code to `puts nil + 10` instead of `8/0`.

If you run this code, it will give the following error:

```
error_handling.rb:1:in `<main>': undefined method `+' for nil:NilClass
(NoMethodError)
```

If you see, the application gives `NoMethodError`, which is exactly what it should be doing because `nil` is not a class defined for the + method.

Also, this error is not caught by the `rescue` block because we are asking it to catch only `ZeroDivisionError`. To catch all standard errors, the code should be like this:

```
rescue StandardError => e
```

Now, if you run this code, the output will be as follows:

```
Error occurred: undefined method `+' for nil:NilClass
```

This is definitely a more descriptive error message and it won't force the application to break.

 Keep in mind that the goal of error handling is not hiding errors, rather it is only for recording them so that you can fix the code implementation.

Developing a custom error logger in Ruby

In this guide, let's wind up error handling in Ruby. In the previous guides, we first looked at the basic error handling syntax and followed that up with a better way to manage errors effectively. In this guide, we will see how we can handle errors in a production application.

We are going to create a method called `error_logger`, which will be responsible for appending all the errors that occur in our program into a log file. Let's create a file called `error_log.txt`. It's an empty file to which we will be adding more data.

This is what our `error_logger` method will look like:

```
def error_logger (e)
  File.open('error-handling-lessons/error_log.txt', 'a') do |file|
    file.puts e
  end
end
```

In this code, we are opening the `error_log.txt` file in the append mode and printing the error message into it. This method takes error as its parameter and puts it into the file.

Next, let's begin our main program code:

```
begin
  puts nil + 10
rescue StandardError => e
  error_logger("Error: #{e} at #{Time.now}")
end
```

If you execute this file, there will be no output visible on the Terminal; however, if you open the `error_log.txt` file, and you will see this error message in it:

```
Error: undefined method `+' for nil:NilClass at 2016-09-05 18:13:29 -0500
```

Now, let's switch up the error by adding the following code in the `begin` portion of the program:

```
puts nil * 10
```

Execute the code and open your log file. You can see that our error log file now has multiple data items:

```
Error: undefined method `+' for nil:NilClass at 2016-09-05 18:13:29 -0500
Error: undefined method `*' for nil:NilClass at 2016-09-05 18:14:09 -0500
```

Let's now attempt to run a divide by 0 operation:

```
puts 8/0
```

The error file will have this message appended as well along with the timestamp of the error:

```
Error: undefined method `+' for nil:NilClass at 2016-09-05 18:13:29 -0500
Error: undefined method `*' for nil:NilClass at 2016-09-05 18:14:09 -0500
Error: divided by 0 at 2016-09-05 18:14:59 -0500
```

So, this is a practical way of handling errors in a real-world program.

Summary

This chapter covered the basic way to handle errors and walked through the proper techniques for implementing error handling in Ruby programs.

You also learned to build an error logging system and saw a practical way of handling errors in a real-world program.

In the next chapter, we'll walk through how to utilize regular expressions in order to implement pattern matching.

12
Regular Expressions in Ruby

In this section of the course, we are going to talk about using regular expressions in Ruby. The goal of this guide is to familiarize you with regular expressions in Ruby and give you the tools necessary to expand your knowledge. As always, we will learn with a practical example that you can use while doing real-world programming.

Pattern matching is a common requirement for building code libraries, such as validations and basic search functionality. In this chapter, we're going to work with regular expressions in Ruby, including the built-in `Regexp` class that allows you to build matchers and dynamically search through data. Additionally, you will be able to:

- Demonstrate how to implement pattern matching in a Ruby program with regular expressions
- Employ different ways in which you can call regular expressions to detect values in string-based values

Regular expression code example

Let's start with some basic regular expression matchers. We'll begin with storing a string sentence in a variable:

```
string = "The quick 12 brown foxes jumped over 10 lazy dogs"
```

First off, let's check whether the preceding string contains the letter o, and to do that, write the following code:

```
p string =~ /o/
```

In Ruby, anything contained within // is a regular expression.

Now if you execute this code, the output should be 15. The value printed out would be 15 because the matcher would find the letter o at position 15.

If you want to find an entire word, you can do that with this code:

```
p string =~ /quick/
```

The output of this will be 4 because the word quick begins at position 4.

A more practical example would be to check whether a letter, say z, is present in a string. If it's present, then it's a valid string; otherwise, it's invalid. To check this, use the following code:

```
p string =~ /z/ ? "Valid" : "Invalid"
```

I'm using a ternary operator for this code. The ternary mechanism allows us to place an if...else condition on the same line. Our preceding ternary code is doing the exact same thing as this:

```
if string =~ /z/
    p "Valid"
else
    p "Invalid"
end
```

So this operator comes in handy because, as you can see, we were able to take five lines of code and combine it into a single line, resulting in the same functionality.

If you execute this program, your output will be "Valid".

Now, let's change it a little bit; replace z with Z:

```
p string =~ /Z/ ? "Valid" : "Invalid"
```

The output will now be "Invalid" because this expression is case-sensitive. To make it case-insensitive, you have to add i to the expression, like this:

```
p string =~ /Z/i ? "Valid" : "Invalid"
```

Now if you execute the code, the output will be "Valid".

The last thing we are going to try is to return all the integer values from the sentence:

```
p string.to_enum(:scan, /\d+/).map {Regexp.last_match}
```

In this code, we are first converting the string into an enumerator and passing the `scan` method to it. This method is part of the library of Ruby's regular expression. Along with it, we are passing a regular expression. The \ expression is the expression that searches for integers, while + looks for multiple instances. If I don't have the + sign, then it will pick only the first integer that it finds. `Regexp` is the class that Ruby has for regular expressions, and `last_match` is one of the methods available in this class.

If you execute this code, the output will be:

```
[#<MatchData "12">, #<MatchData "10">]
```

This is perfect because we have only two integers—10 and 12—in the string, which is what the preceding code printed out.

So, with just one line of code, we were able to scan the string, pick integers, and display their respective values.

I think you're going to enjoy this guide since we are going to walk through a practical example of using regular expressions. In this guide, we are going to check whether a particular string is a valid email address or not. In fact, I pulled this out of one of my Rails applications so you can get a hands-on feel of Ruby programming in a real-world program.

Regex code example

To start, let's create a constant variable that will store our regular expression. I'm not going to go into detail to describe how each expression works because this is not a regular expression course (and entire books have been written dedicated solely to regular expressions). Instead, we'll focus on how to use them in Ruby. There are countless resources with regex cheat sheets that you can incorporate for matchers.

Here is the regular expression code that will verify that a string matches the common pattern, followed by email addresses:

```
VALID_EMAIL_REGEX = /\A([\w+\-].?)+@[a-z\d\-]+(\.[a-z]+)*\.[a-z]+\z/i
```

If you look at this expression, the first part allows names, numbers, dashes, and dots. This is followed by ensuring that the @ symbol is used. Next, it verifies that letters and numbers follow the @ symbol. This is followed by . and letters. So, this is typically in the something@domain.extension format. At the end, we are ensuring that the matcher is case-insensitive with /i.

Next, we are going to build a method that will verify this pattern:

```
def is_valid_email? email
    email =~ VALID_EMAIL_REGEX
end
```

In this code, we are creating a method called is_valid_email? and passing an argument called email.

Next, we are checking this parameter against the VALID_EMAIL_REGEX constant to return either true or false.

Let's check some use cases now:

```
p is_valid_email?("jordan@hudgens.com") ? "Valid" : "Invalid"
p is_valid_email?("jordanhudgens.com") ? "Valid" : "Invalid"
p is_valid_email?("jordan.h@hudgens.com") ? "Valid" : "Invalid"
p is_valid_email?("jordan@hudgens") ? "Valid" : "Invalid"
```

If you execute this code, your output should be:

```
"Valid"
"Invalid"
"Valid"
"Invalid"
```

So, the first and third email addresses are valid because they match our pattern, while the second and fourth are invalid.

 When you use a ternary operator, you have to enclose your arguments in parentheses.

Let's try one more use case:

```
p is_valid_email?("jordan_h@hudgens.net") ? "Valid" : "Invalid"
```

If you run it, the output will be "Valid", so the application does accept the _ symbol in addition to dashes.

This is how you can integrate your regular expression email validator code in a Ruby on Rails application:

```
1  class Job < ActiveRecord::Base
2    validates_presence_of :req_number, :title, :city, :state, :description, :requi
3    has_many :job_applications
4
5    validate :has_valid_email?
6
7    VALID_EMAIL_REGEX = /\A([\w+\-].?)+@[a-z\d\-]+(\.[a-z]+)*\.[a-z]+\z/i
8
9    def has_valid_email?
10     self.email =~ VALID_EMAIL_REGEX
11   end
12 end
```

Therefore, by leveraging regular expressions, we can do something complex, such as checking an email address with only a few lines of code. Without regular expressions, you would probably be writing hundreds of lines of code to check against every possibility.

How to validate an IP address using regular expressions

Now we'll build an IP matcher using Ruby and regular expressions. An example of how this could be used would be through building a security module that either verifies or blocks IP addresses in a program.

To do this, let's define a constant that will store the regular expression:

```
IP_ADDRESS_REGEX =
/^((?:(?:^|\.)(?:\d|[1-9]\d|1\d{2}|2[0-4]\d|25[0-5])){4})$/
```

This regular expression will take all the valid IP address values, which range from `172.16.0.0` to `172.31.255.255`.

The rest of the code is going to be fairly similar to the `validator` email address:

```
def is_valid_ip_address? ip
  ip =~ IP_ADDRESS_REGEX
end
```

Next, let's check some use cases:

```
p is_valid_ip_address? ("999.16.0.0") ? "Valid" : "Invalid"
p is_valid_ip_address? ("172.16.0.0") ? "Valid" : "Invalid"
p is_valid_ip_address? ("172.31.255.255") ? "Valid" : "Invalid"
p is_valid_ip_address? ("172.31.255.256") ? "Valid" : "Invalid"
```

If you execute this code, your output will be:

```
"Invalid"
"Valid"
"Valid"
"Invalid"
```

That's the right output based on the sample data.

When working with regular expressions, I find it helpful to use a tool called *Rubular*. Go to `rubular.com`; you'll find it's a pretty handy tool to create regular expressions in Ruby.

To test how these values work in Rubular, copy the regular expression and paste it on the web page. Also, copy each one of the use cases and paste it to the **Your test string** column. If it is a valid string, it should look like this:

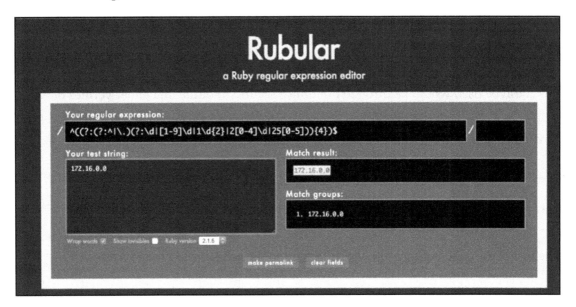

If it is not a valid string, then the output would be as follows:

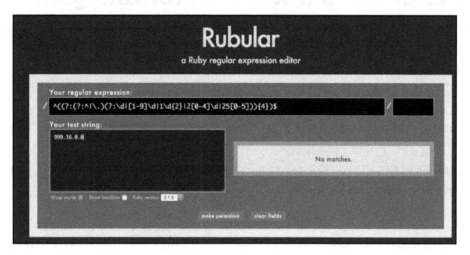

This tool can be a great way to run different test strings. You can also experiment with various regular expressions to get the results you want. There are also some quick reference expressions in the lower part of the page that you can use:

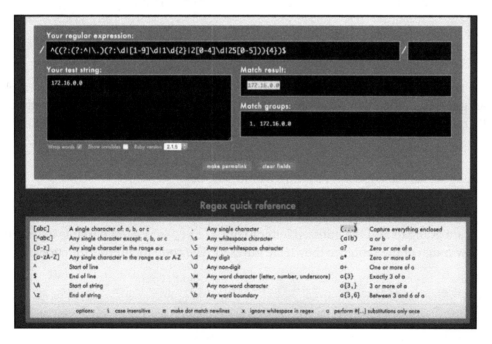

How to develop a wheel of fortune game

This is going to be a fun lesson since we are going to build a *Wheel of Fortune* guessing game using regular expressions and several other Ruby methods.

To start out, let's create a variable called:

```
starting_sentence = "Hi from matching land"
```

This variable is the sentence that the user is going to have to guess while playing the *Wheel of Fortune* game.

The next step is to convert the sentence into an array of letters and convert them all into lowercase letters. The code for this is:

```
sentence_array = starting_sentence.split("").map(&:downcase)
```

Next, we have to get the count of letters in the array minus the empty spaces; to do this, add the following code:

```
accurate_count = sentence_array - [" "]
```

This value will be useful to loop through `sentence_array` later.

Then, we put our regular expression through the `gsub` method:

```
final_sentence = starting_sentence.gsub(/[a-zA-Z]/, "_").split("")
```

Now we are going to convert letters into empty spaces as they are guessed. For example, if the user guesses `l`, then that position would be converted into an empty space without actually removing that letter from the array. To visualize, our array would start like this:

```
["H", "i", "f", "r"...]
```

If the user guesses the `r` letter, our string would now be:

```
["H", "i", "f", ""...]
```

Also, we are going to add the guessed letter to our `final_sentence` variable to let the user know how much of the sentence they have guessed. The code for all this functionality is:

```
while sentence_array.count("") < accurate_count.count
  puts "Guess a letter"
  guess = gets.downcase.chomp
  if sentence_array.include?(guess)
    letter_index = sentence_array.find_index(guess)
    sentence_array[letter_index] = ""
```

```
      final_sentence[letter_index] = guess
      puts "Correct! The sentence is now: #{final_sentence.join}"
   else
      puts "Sorry, that letter isn't the right answer, please try again."
   end
 end
```

In this code, we are using a `while` loop to check whether the empty spaces in the `sentence_array` variable are less than `accurate_count`. We want the loop to end when all the letters are guessed, which means that it's nothing more than an array of empty spaces. In other words, when `sentence_array` has only empty spaces, our loop should end.

Next, we prompted the user to enter a letter, and we get the input and store it in a variable called `guess`.

Then, we have a conditional, and for this, we used a method called `include`. This method is fairly similar to the `gsub` method, but `include` is better when we want to find values in an array. Essentially, this function checks the input parameter with all the values in the array and proceeds to the next line if there is a match. If the letter that is guessed is not in the sentence, then the application moves to the `else` block.

Our code inside of the `if` block finds the position of the particular letter in the array. We store this index value in a variable called `letter_index`. For example, if the user guesses the letter i, the `find_array` method will look through the array and return position 1 to the `letter_index` variable. Remember, array positions start at 0, so the second letter would be at position 1.

Now that we know the position of the guessed letter in the array, we set it to an empty string in the next line of code.

Next, we set the value of our input letter to the `letter_index` position of the `final_sentence` array. Lastly, we displayed a message along with the sentence's `final_sentence` variable to let the users know how much of the sentence they have completed. The `join` method there converts the array into a sentence.

If the preceding condition is not true, then the application executes the `else` block, where we ask the user to input another letter.

Now if you execute this code, it will allow us to play the game.

If you notice, all the letters are replaced by the _ symbol when the game starts. This code took the value from `starting_sentence` and substituted all the uppercase and lowercase alphabets with _.

So how do the letters know their respective positions? If you go back to the code, you will find the position of each letter from the orie `letter_index` variable.

To test case sensitivity, we guessed the lowercase letter h. In the output, you can see that the application placed it at the right spot, which is at the beginning of the sentence.

Now try a letter that's not in the string, say z. The output would be:

```
Sorry, that letter isn't the right answer, please try again.
```

You can continue guessing letters until the sentence is complete to have some fun.

Lastly, let's check whether our `while` loop has ended correctly. So, continue guessing all the letters. When you guess the last letter, the application comes out of the loop, as you will be able to see in the output.

Hopefully, that was a fun learning experience. Play around with this code a little bit to get a better understanding. As an exercise, see how you can refactor the program to make it more efficient.

Summary

In this chapter, you were introduced to how Ruby implements regular expressions. We saw how to build a custom email validation program by leveraging regular expressions. We also examined how to build an IP address validation tool.

We discussed tools, such as *Rubular*, that are utilized regularly by the Ruby community when building and testing regular expression matchers. We also had fun building a *Wheel of Fortune* game that integrates regex matchers combined with other Ruby string methods.

In the next chapter, we're going to walk through how to leverage the `grep` method in Ruby programs.

13
Searching with grep in Ruby

Ruby offers a wide variety of options when it comes to searching through strings. In this chapter, you'll learn how to use the powerful `grep` method in Ruby programs to search through data. Additionally, you'll be able to:

- Demonstrate how to implement the `grep` method in order to match designated patterns in a string
- Show how to combine regular expressions with `grep` to find values

How to use grep in Ruby

In this section, we are going to learn more about a powerful method in Ruby called `grep`. This method is used to easily search through arrays and other collections.

We are going to learn the use of this method in a real-world Rails application.

If I go to the root of the application in the Terminal, I can run the `rake routes` command to get a list of all the routes in the application.

This will display all the different routes in the application, as follows:

This is helpful but also a bit overwhelming. What if I wanted only the routes specific to `posts`? So to filter this list, I can use the `grep` method. Just run the following command in the Terminal:

```
rake routes | grep posts
```

The output will be much more manageable:

When you use this command, it only brings up all the routes that have the word `posts` in them.

So what does `grep` do exactly?

Let's see a simple example:

```
arr = [1, 3, 2, 12, 1, 2, 3]
p arr.grep(1)
```

In this code, we have a basic array of integers. From here, we call the `grep` method on the array and pass in the value that we want to search for, in this case, `1`. The output will be an array containing two instances of `1`:

```
[1, 1]
```

Now if you search for `100` with `grep(100)`, it will return an empty array because there are no array elements of `100`.

So, `grep` is an elegant and easy way to search through collections. Keep in mind you wouldn't use `grep` to search through a database or anything of that size since you'd run into performance issues; however, it's great for smaller collections.

How to use grep instead of the select and map methods

This section will teach you how to use `grep` instead of other methods in Ruby, such as `select` and `map`, to search through a collection.

To start with, I'm going to create an array of filenames, as shown in the following code:

```
arr = ['hey.rb', 'there.rb', 'index.html']
```

Now let's see how we can use `grep` to perform the functions of `select` or `map`.

First, let's say you want to return only the files that end in the extension `.rb`, and along with it, you want to remove the extension so the output has only filenames.

The typical code to implement this type of behavior would be something like this:

```
p arr.select { |x| x=~ /\.rb/ }.map{ |x| x[0..-4]}
```

The output should just have the `["hey", "there"]` values.

Though it worked, we can make it more efficient using the `grep` method. By leveraging `grep`, our code can be consolidated down to:

```
arr.grep(/(.*)\.rb/){$1}
```

The output will be the same.

 The {$1} expression is a tool that you can use with regular expression matchers in Ruby to capture the values that were matched. So, in our example, the actual values that were matched were hey and there. The .rb extension was left off by default because it was not part of the match value that was returned. Ruby borrowed this concept from the Perl programming language.

Summary

In summary, we saw how grep is an elegant and easy way to search through small collections. We also walked through how grep can be utilized in place of various other Ruby methods, such as select.

In the next chapter, we're going to analyze how to work with external code libraries, specifically Ruby gems.

14
Ruby Gems

One of the reasons for Ruby's growth in popularity over the past decade is due to the open source community building code libraries that can be implemented in other applications. Typically, these code libraries are called **Ruby gems**. In this chapter, you'll walk through and learn what Ruby gems are, how to use them, and where you can find new gems to give your Ruby programs additional functionality. By the end of this chapter, you will be able to:

- Demonstrate how to integrate third-party code libraries
- Employ Ruby gems to add additional functionality to Ruby programs

Introduction to Ruby gems

In this chapter, we are going to talk about an exciting and important topic called Ruby gems. Gems are modules and classes that provide additional functionality to an application. Some gems provide so many features that individuals new to development may even think of them like some kind of programming magic. However, essentially, gems are nothing more than Ruby code files that perform certain tasks.

To give you an idea of how gems are used, I'm going to open Gemfile in a Rails project:

```
source 'https://rubygems.org'

gem 'rails', '~> 5.0', '>= 5.0.0.1'
gem 'pg', '~> 0.15'
gem 'sass-rails', '~> 5.0'
gem 'uglifier', '>= 1.3.0'
gem 'coffee-rails', '~> 4.1.0'
gem 'jquery-rails'
gem 'turbolinks'
gem 'jbuilder', '~> 2.0'
```

```
gem 'sdoc', '~> 0.4.0', group: :doc

group :development, :test do
  gem 'byebug'
  gem 'rspec-rails', '~> 3.0'
  gem 'capybara'
  gem 'database_cleaner'
  gem 'factory_girl_rails', '~> 4.7'
end

group :development do
  gem 'web-console', '~> 2.0'
  gem 'spring'
end

gem 'devise', '~> 4.2'
gem 'bootstrap-sass', '~> 3.3', '>= 3.3.6'
gem "gritter", "1.2.0"
gem 'administrate', github: 'greetpoint/administrate', branch: 'rails5'
gem 'bourbon'
gem 'pundit', '~> 1.1'
gem 'puma', '~> 3.4'
gem 'twilio-ruby', '~> 4.11', '>= 4.11.1'
gem 'dotenv-rails', :groups => [:development, :test]
gem 'kaminari', '~> 0.17.0'
gem 'rails_12factor'
gem 'honeybadger', '~> 2.0'
gem 'newrelic_rpm', '~> 3.15', '>= 3.15.0.314'
```

Each of these gems contains a set of modules that allows programs to use them, so you don't have to write every feature in an application from scratch. Using gems can save you quite a bit of time and effort so that you don't have to reinvent the wheel every time. There are thousands of gems available for you, and I recommend that you go to RubyGems.org (h ttps://rubygems.org/) to look at the full directory.

Let's walk through a few of the features that the gems from the code in this section provide:

- rspec (https://rails.devcamp.com/ruby-gem-walkthroughs/testing-gems /rspec-rails-gem-tutorial): This provides a fully automated BDD test framework for applications
- devise (https://rails.devcamp.com/trails/ruby-gem-walkthroughs/camps ites/authentication/guides/devise): This allows you to create a full authentication feature

- kaminari (https://rails.devcamp.com/ruby-gem-walkthroughs/view-templ ate-tools/kaminari-pagination-example): This enables you to implement pagination anywhere it's needed in an application
- pundit (https://rails.devcamp.com/professional-rails-development-cou rse/post-feature/integrating-basic-authorization-in-rails): This gives developers the ability to build a full permission structure to ensure users follow the correct authorization rules

I hope this gives you an idea of the power of Ruby gems and how they can practically be used in a real-world application.

How to research Ruby gems

In this section, I'm going to show you how to research Ruby gems. The main repository for gems can be found at Rubygems.org (https://rubygems.org/):

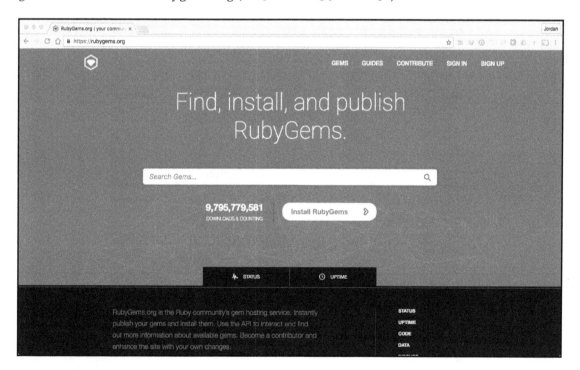

On this site, you can find all kinds of gems. Additionally, you can refer to locations, such as GitHub (`https://github.com/`), to find new gems. However, it is considered a best practice to get gems from RubyGems.org because the site has the most up-to-date gems and versions. There are times when developers forget to update their GitHub repositories, which can result in version conflicts.

How to research gems

To get started, I'm going to search for a gem called `pundit`.

This will bring up the following search results for you:

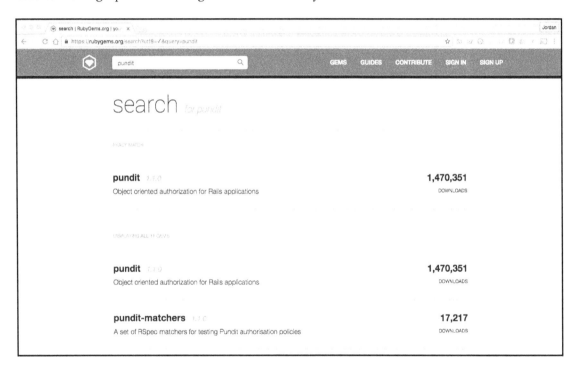

If you click on the first link, it will take you to a page that has all the information needed to research the gem:

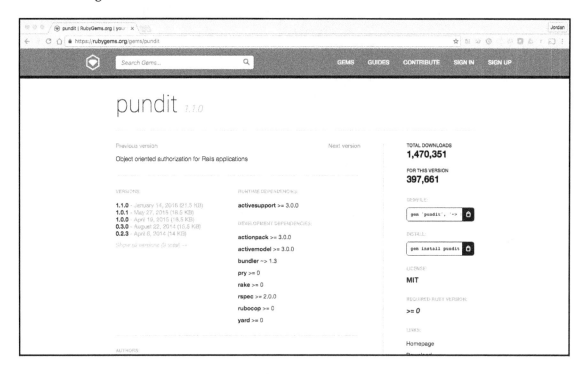

You can see how popular a gem is by looking at the number of times it has been downloaded. Also, this page shows the number of times that a particular version was downloaded, which is important when you're analyzing different gem versions. Just below the download statistics, you can see the code that you can paste into your application. When you use the RubyGems.org site, this code also comes with the stable version number embedded in the code itself, which is quite helpful.

If you look in the middle of the page, you can see the full list of outside dependencies that the gem has. What this means is when you install `pundit`, it will install all these dependencies too. Knowing this information is important because sometimes, you'll run into a situation where a gem has a conflict with another gem and the cause of the issue was one of the dependencies. For example, if you bring in the `will_paginate` gem (`https://r ails.devcamp.com/ruby-gem-walkthroughs/view-template-tools/will-paginate-exa mple`), there may be a conflict with `rails_admin` (`https://rails.devcamp.com/ruby-gem -walkthroughs/admin-dashboard-gems/rails-admin-gem-tutorial`), something I've run into on several occasions.

If you scroll down the page, you will see some links on the right-hand side. The most important link is the home page as it takes you to the corresponding gem page, which is usually on GitHub. This link contains information on how to install and use the particular gem.

Other than this, this page has information about past versions, contributors, and other information that may be helpful.

Summary

In this chapter, we took an introductory look at Ruby gems and how they can be utilized in a program to extend the functionality of an application. We also saw how you can research a gem to find how popular it is, when it was last updated, and various other data points to help you decide whether the gem is the right fit for your program.

In the next chapter, we're going to walk through how to implement metaprogramming in a Ruby program.

15
Ruby Metaprogramming

Writing code that writes code is one of the more challenging topics in any programming language. However, metaprogramming in Ruby offers a powerful interface for building advanced features into an application; it is worth the effort to learn it. In this chapter, you will learn some of the basics of metaprogramming in Ruby, including how to open classes and add functionality to built-in Ruby classes. Additionally, you will be able to:

- Demonstrate what metaprogramming is and how it can be implemented in Ruby
- Analyze how to build programs that write code by leveraging methods, such as `method missing` and `define_method`

Metaprogramming introduction

We will start learning about metaprogramming in Ruby. Let's begin with a practical example. Refer to the following screenshot:

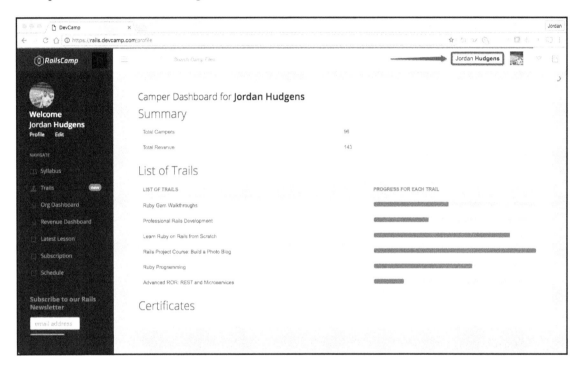

This is a profile page for `devcamp.com`. You can see my full name listed on the top right-hand side. This name was collected by the application when I signed up, and when I logged in later, it was retrieved from the database and displayed.

To display this value, you can update your `User` class in the application and override the built-in `to_s` string method, like so:

```
def to_s
  self.first_name + " " + self.last_name
end
```

Now if you call the `to_s` method on any objects created from the `User` class, you'll get the full name value.

So metaprogramming gives us the ability to open up classes and override existing methods to assign custom behavior to applications. This is by no means the full scope of what metaprogramming offers, but it's an introduction to how you can easily use it in your applications.

How to integrate metaprogramming techniques into a custom class

Now that you have gone through the *Metaprogramming introduction* section, let's see how to integrate it into a custom class in Ruby.

To start, let's create an empty `Baseball` class:

```
class Baseball
end
```

Now, we instantiate it and call a method using the following code:

```
p Baseball.new.swing
```

You'll get an error, and this is good because we don't have a method called `swing` in the `Baseball` class.

In a later lesson, we'll walk through the process of creating methods on the fly, but right now, let's simply open the `Baseball` class and add the method manually:

```
class Baseball
end

class Baseball
  def swing
    "Homerun"
  end
end

p Baseball.new.swing
```

If you run this program, it will return the `"Homerun"` message. This example shows the flexibility that Ruby offers when you want to reopen a class and make changes to it. Since this is a basic example, it doesn't make much of a difference. But if you have to do this in a large Ruby program with hundreds of files, then this type of flexibility is very beneficial.

Returning to our `Baseball` class, we even have the ability to open it again to override the `swing` method, like so:

```
class Baseball
end

class Baseball
  def swing
    "Homerun"
  end
end

p Baseball.new.swing # > Homerun

class Baseball
  def swing
    "Strike"
  end
end

p Baseball.new.swing  # > Strike
```

If you execute this method, the output of the second `swing` call would be `"Strike"`.

Hope this gives you a good idea of metaprogramming in Ruby. This still only focuses on opening and closing classes. In future sections, we'll walk through how `method_missing` works, which is the core component utilized in Ruby metaprogramming. That being said, when it comes to day-to-day development, I probably use the process of opening and closing classes more than any other metaprogramming tool.

How to use metaprogramming for opening and customizing the String class

In the *How to integrate metaprogramming techniques into a custom class* section, we went through a basic example of metaprogramming just to get an idea of what it is and how we can use it. In this section, let's see a more practical way of using it.

In this case, we'll open the `String` class in Ruby. This is a core Ruby class that is used extensively. For example, every time you declare a variable with a string value, you instantiate an object of the `String` class.

Now when we define a class called `String`, remember that we're simply reopening this class; we're not creating one from scratch. Let's add a method called `censor` to block out certain words in an application. Currently, the `String` class has no such method, so we'll not override any preexisting methods. The code will look like this:

```
class String
  def censor(bad_word)
    self.gsub! "#{bad_word}", "CENSORED"
  end
end
```

In this code, we called `self` because we wanted any string to be able to call this method onto itself. We called the `gsub` method and performed some string interpolation, which will swap a replacement word instead of the banned word. Essentially, this code will replace the word that gets passed to the `censor` method with the `CENSORED` word.

Now, to test it, let's add a sentence that we call the method on:

```
p "The bunny was in trouble with the king's bunny".censor('bunny')
```

Running the program will produce this output:

```
"The CENSORED was in trouble with the king's CENSORED"
```

Now, let's add a new method that gives a same result as the pre-existing piece of functionality will. The `String` class already has a method called `size`:

```
p "The bunny was in trouble with the king's bunny".size
```

If we run this method on our string, it will produce the following output:

```
# > 46
```

However, what if we want to be able to create a more explicit method name for this feature? We can open up the `String` class again with this code:

```
class String
  def num_of_chars
    size
  end
end

p "The bunny was in trouble with the king's bunny".num_of_chars
```

If you run this code, you'll see that we get an output identical to when we use the `size` method directly. I admit this example isn't very practical since the `size` method is more succinct and works quite well. However, it's a feature of Ruby that you may need to use at some point, so it's a good skill to learn.

The nice thing about opening built-in classes, such as the `String` class, is that you're able to add custom behavior that can be called directly on objects, such as sentences.

How Rails use metaprogramming for the find_by method

So far, we have seen:

- A basic overview of metaprogramming
- How we can use it in a custom class
- How to use it on existing Ruby classes, such as the `String` class

In this section, we are going to see how metaprogramming can be used in real-world applications.

I'm going to open up a Ruby on Rails application because Rails leverages metaprogramming as well as any program I've ever seen. We're going to walk through how the Rails framework generates database lookup methods on the fly.

Here is the database schema file for the Rails application we're going to look at:

```
create_table "contacts", force: true do |t|
  t.string   "name"
  t.string   "email"
  t.text     "message"
  t.string   "category"
  t.datetime "created_at"
  t.datetime "updated_at"
end

create_table "customers", force: true do |t|
  t.string   "name"
  t.datetime "created_at"
  t.datetime "updated_at"
  t.string   "email"
  t.text     "logo"
end
```

```
create_table "location_posts", force: true do |t|
  t.integer  "post_id"
  t.integer  "location_id"
  t.datetime "created_at"
  t.datetime "updated_at"
end
```

We're going to use the `customers` table as our case study for this section.

In the Rails console (which gives us the ability to perform database queries), you can bring up the record of the last customer with the `Customer.last` command:

What happens if we only know the name of the customer and have no other details and we want to pull up a record based on the name?

To do that, the command is:

```
Customer.find_by_name("Warren Cat")
```

If you run this code, you'll see that it returns the same record as before.

The cool thing about this method is that Rails only has a method called `find_by`, and it uses metaprogramming to allow users to dynamically enter the database's field. In this sense, "name" is simply an argument for the `find_by` method, though it may look like a complete method by itself.

If you go to the Rails source code, you can see this method:

```
# Finds the first record matching the specified conditions. There
# is no implied ordering so if order matters, you should specify it
# yourself.
#
# If no record is found, returns <tt>nil</tt>.
#
#   Post.find_by name: 'Spartacus', rating: 4
#   Post.find_by "published_at< ?", 2.weeks.ago
def find_by(arg, *args)
  where(arg, *args).take
rescue RangeError
  nil
end
```

You can see that this method references the first argument and it takes on any number of arguments.

Now, to prove that the find_by method takes other parameters too, let's pull up a record based on email:

```
Customer.find_by_email("yadeco2@yahoo.com")
```

The output brings up the exact same record. Let's take this a bit further; let's look at the second table in our preceding list of tables, which is location. There is no name attribute in this table at all. So, if you use name here, it will throw an error. The command would be:

```
Location.find_by_name("Midland")
```

The application throws an `undefined method` error:

```
●  ●  ●                    crudelist — node • heroku run rails c — 80×24
                    ~/code/crudelist — node • heroku run rails c                              +
Loading production environment (Rails 4.0.2)
irb(main):001:0> Customer.last
=> #<Customer id: 7, name: "Warren Cat", created_at: "2015-04-10 20:05:29", upda
ted_at: "2015-04-10 20:05:29", email: "yadeco2@yahoo.com">
irb(main):002:0> Customer.find_by_name("Warren Cat")
=> #<Customer id: 7, name: "Warren Cat", created_at: "2015-04-10 20:05:29", upda
ted_at: "2015-04-10 20:05:29", email: "yadeco2@yahoo.com">
irb(main):003:0> Customer.find_by_email("yadeco2@yahoo.com")
=> #<Customer id: 7, name: "Warren Cat", created_at: "2015-04-10 20:05:29", upda
ted_at: "2015-04-10 20:05:29", email: "yadeco2@yahoo.com">
irb(main):004:0> Location.find_by_name("Midland")
NoMethodError: undefined method `find_by_name' for #<Class:0x007fcc65555968>
        from /app/vendor/bundle/ruby/2.0.0/gems/activerecord-4.0.2/lib/active_re
cord/dynamic_matchers.rb:22:in `method_missing'
        from (irb):4
        from /app/vendor/bundle/ruby/2.0.0/gems/railties-4.0.2/lib/rails/command
s/console.rb:90:in `start'
        from /app/vendor/bundle/ruby/2.0.0/gems/railties-4.0.2/lib/rails/command
s/console.rb:9:in `start'
        from /app/vendor/bundle/ruby/2.0.0/gems/railties-4.0.2/lib/rails/command
s.rb:62:in `<top (required)>'
        from /app/bin/rails:4:in `require'
        from /app/bin/rails:4:in `<main>'
irb(main):005:0> █
```

Rails is intelligent enough to know that it can only utilize existing attributes for its `find_by` method and not just any random attribute.

This goes to show that `find_by_name` is not a method by itself; rather; Rails takes the first argument and creates a method dynamically using metaprogramming. You may also have noticed that I circled the `method_missing` message in the Terminal. The `method_missing` message is going to be a topic that we're going to explore in future guides. As I've mentioned earlier, `method_missing` is the core component that allows for Ruby's most powerful metaprogramming features.

Utilizing metaprogramming with method_missing to create methods on the fly

This will be an interesting section. You are going to learn how to create code that will write code inside a Ruby program by leveraging the metaprogramming construct of `method_missing`. Though it's an advanced Ruby concept, it's fun to learn and I think it'll be handy for you. So let's get started.

Imagine we have a database called `Author`, and, in it, we have different attributes, such as `first_name`, `last_name`, and `genre`. What do we do if we want to create dynamic methods on the fly? For example, if we create a new author in the database, we want custom methods to print out each of the attributes. At the same time, we don't want to hardcode a bunch of methods; we want them to get generated dynamically. Essentially, we want a metaprogramming method that will write code dynamically on the fly based on the arguments sent to it.

Let's see how to do that:

```
require 'ostruct'

class Author
  attr_accessor :first_name, :last_name, :genre

  def author
    OpenStruct.new(first_name: first_name, last_name: last_name,
    genre: genre)
  end

  def method_missing(method_name, *arguments, &block)
    if method_name.to_s =~ /author_(.*)/
      author.send($1, *arguments, &block)
    else
      super
    end
  end
end

author = Author.new
author.first_name = "Cal"
author.last_name = "Newpot"
author.genre = "Computer Science"
```

Let's walk through the code line by line.

In the first line, we included a library that'll give us access to some methods. In this code, we used it as a data structure to mimic a database, since creating a database and populating it would take up too much time.

Next, we created a class called `Author` and defined attributes for it. In the next line, we created a method called `author`, and, inside it, we created an `OpenStruct` object with values for each attribute. Essentially, this will function like a database.

Next, we used a key method called `method_missing` that is built into Ruby. In this sense, we did not create a new method but overrode an existing method. It takes three arguments, namely:

- A method name
- An array of arguments
- A code block

Inside this method, we place a condition to check whether the method name that was passed starts with `author_`. As you can see, if it does, we call the `author` method and send arguments to it. The argument `$1` grabs the first element in the argument array, `*arguments` passes the remaining arguments, and `&block` passes the block of code.

If this condition fails, we call `super`, as we want the code to just call the parent class. Since we haven't inherited from any other class, Ruby will look for this method in the `BasicObject` class and will do nothing with it.

Why do we need to call super?

Let's say we have a method that does not start with `author_`. In that case, we tell Ruby that we don't have any code for such a method. In other words, we want Ruby to generate methods only for those values that start with `author_` and not for other methods.

To check whether this code works, let's instantiate `Author`. We will create a new variable called `author` and set attributes for this object.

Let's test it out. Before that, let's print out our author's first name to know whether the program is working fine. We add this piece of code to establish a base case:

```
p author.first_name
```

The output will be as follows:

```
"Cal"
```

That's right!

Now, let's see what happens if we change it to:

```
p author.author_genre
```

The output is `"Computer Science"`.

So we have successfully implemented a full metaprogramming module for our `Author` class.

As you can see, we don't have a method called `author_genre`, yet it returned the right value because this method was created on the fly by `method_missing`. This is an important method to know as it can give you quite a bit of flexibility while building out Ruby programs.

One important thing I want to show you is the `respond_to?` method. This method comes by default with all the functioning methods and it checks whether a particular method exists in the code.

Here's an example:

```
p author.respond_to?(:inspect)
```

This will return the value `true` because `inspect` comes for all objects by default. On the other hand, suppose we say:

```
p author.respond_to?(:author_genre)
```

It returns the value `false` because this method is not present in the code.

This is a potential problem because many programmers will put `respond_to?` in a conditional to check whether a particular method exists before executing the remaining code. They will do this just to ensure that the program works. In the next section, we'll see how to overcome this drawback.

Resources

The code for this section is available at `https://github.com/rails-camp/ruby-programming/blob/master/mmissing.rb`.

Incorporating respond_to_missing to conform to metaprogramming best practices

In the previous section, you learned about a metaprogramming method called method_missing.

As mentioned earlier, the problem with this method is that most developers tend to use the respond_to? method to check whether the method is present and, only if the value is true, the rest of the code is executed. To ensure that we're conforming to Ruby best practices, override the respond_to? method, like so:

```
def respond_to_missing?(method_name, include_private = false)
  method_name.to_s.start_with?('author_') || super
end
```

In this code, we passed two arguments to the method and, in the next line, we created a conditional that is similar to the one in method_missing. However, we are using a different syntax to get more familiar with different syntaxes.

Instead of using an if...else statement, we simply execute the same functionality on a single line. This code first converts the method_name into a string and checks whether it starts with the word author_. If so, it returns the value true; otherwise, it returns false.

Though this syntax is much shorter, it won't work so well in the method_missing method. In that method, we send a value, whereas, here, we simply check for the presence of a certain word. So, even if we can technically write the code in a single line in method_missing, it might look confusing. I have no qualms writing three lines of code instead of one if it results in the code being more explicit and easier to understand.

When we run this code, the output is:

```
"Computer Science"
true
```

You can see the method has returned the value true, and this is in tune with the established programming practices.

You can now use this code as a template when you do metaprogramming in future.

Resources

The code for this section is available at `https://github.com/rails-camp/ruby-programming/blob/master/respond_to.rb`.

Implementing metaprogramming with define_method

In this section, you'll learn about another metaprogramming mechanism called `define_method` that will allow you to dynamically create methods at runtime in a Ruby program.

We'll continue with our `Author` class and use a method called `define_method` here:

```
class Author
  define_method("some_method") do
    puts "Some details"
  end
end
```

Next, we'll call this method:

```
author = Author.new
author.some_method
```

When you run this code, it'll print out the `Some details` value.

You may wonder how this is different from a regular method, such as this one:

```
def some_method
  puts "Some details"
end
```

The answer is, they are the same!

So, this is not the kind of implementation you'd use `define_method` for in the real world. However, I wanted to start with this as a base case so you can see the core functionality.

Now let's look at a more practical example. Going back to our `Author` class, let's imagine that we have different genres and we have to print out the details of each of the different genres. To do that, let's create a few methods inside our `Author` class, like so:

```
class Author
  def fiction_details(arg)
    puts "fiction"
```

```
    puts arg
    puts "something else..."
  end

  def coding_details(arg)
    puts "coding"
    puts arg
    puts "something else..."
  end

  def history_details(arg)
    puts "history"
    puts arg
    puts "something else..."
  end
end
```

Each of these methods simply prints out the values based on the arguments that are passed to it. Let's call one of the methods now with the code:

```
author = Author.new
author.coding_details("Cal Newport")
```

When you run this code, it will print out:

coding
Cal Newport
something else...

Though this implementation works, it showcases some poor programming practices because of the amount of identical code we are using. This is where define_method is useful. A better implementation would be to utilize define_method, which would look something like this:

```
class Author
  genres = %w(fiction coding history)

  genres.each do |genre|
    define_method("#{genre}_details") do |arg|
      puts "Genre: #{genre}"
      puts arg
      puts genre.object_id
    end
  end
end

author = Author.new
author.coding_details "Cal Newport"
```

In this code, we created a variable called `genres`. If you're not familiar with the `%w(...)` syntax, it is a way that Ruby allows us to create an array of strings without commas and double quotes. In the next line, we iterated over the `genres` array, and inside `each` block, we called `define_method`. Inside this block, we printed the name of the genre and the value of `arg`. Lastly, we generated a unique ID with the `genre.object_id` code to show that the object values will be unique.

Essentially, what this code does is it iterates over our `genres` array and, based on the genre, it dynamically creates a method that will have the name of the genre, followed by the word `_details`. If you notice, the functionality is the same as before, but this time, we have to define it only once, and obviously, the amount of code is greatly reduced.

Now if you run the code, the output will be:

```
Genre: coding
Cal Newport
70338847194560
```

Let's add another line:

```
author.fiction_details("Ayn Rand")
```

And now the result is:

```
Genre: coding
Cal Newport
70107179007240
Genre: fiction
Ayn Rand
70107179007260
```

So, everything's working fine. See how easy and compact your code is when you use `define_method`?

There's also another cool thing about this method. If you remember, in the *Utilizing metaprogramming with method_missing to create methods on the fly* section, we had to integrate our `respond_to?` method to get it to work properly? You can call that method here, like this:

```
p author.respond_to?("coding_details")
```

When you execute it, the program will output `true`.

In the *Utilizing metaprogramming with method_missing to create methods on the fly* section, we had to build another method simply to ensure that the `respond_to?` method would work properly (which is the key to us following best practices for metaprogramming). However, when we use `define_method`, it actually creates methods for us at runtime; the `respond_to?` method comes by default.

At this point, I'd like to point out a subtle difference that exists between the `define_method` and `method_missing` methods in Ruby. Since `define_method` creates the methods for us at runtime, we get the functionality of the `respond_to?` method for free. On the other hand, the `method_missing` method does not trigger a call until the method call has gone through the method call cycle with Ruby. For example, let's say we had a call for a method named `summary`, like this:

```
author.summary
```

Ruby will go to the `Author` class and look for a method called `summary`. When it can't find it there, it'll go up the chain and look for this method in `BasicObject` and all the other built-in classes that Ruby has to check to see whether there is a `summary` method somewhere that it can call. When Ruby can't find the method anywhere, it comes back to the `Author` class and checks to confirm whether there is a `method_missing` definition and whether there is a `summary` method in it. This is why we had to add the `respond_to?` method earlier in order to get it working. With `define_method`, we don't have to write any code for `respond_to?` as it works right out of the box for us.

However, the downside with `define_method` is its limited flexibility. With `method_missing`, you can do pretty much anything when there is a method call for a non-existent method, but with `define_method`, you can't do anything other than defining methods from a predefined list of values. Also, we have to provide all the necessary details at the time of writing the code to ensure that `define_method` works properly. However, with `missing_method`, you can decide what you want to do when the call comes in at runtime.

In short, you can use `define_method` when you know what needs to be done. In fact, it's key use is to create methods for you at runtime based on the details you provide in the code, just like how we did. In this sense, it's a great way to DRY up your code and have a nice code structure.

Resources

The code file for this is available at `https://github.com/rails-camp/ruby-programming/blob/master/dmethod.rb`.

Summary

Metaprogramming gives us the ability to open up classes and override existing methods or add new methods in order to assign custom behavior to applications. We walked through how metaprogramming can be utilized in programs to dynamically build methods on the fly. This can provide developers with a custom interface to your code in the way that Rails allows you to use custom query methods. We also saw how to build our own metaprogramming component.

We analyzed how to utilize `method_missing` in a Ruby program to generate methods on the fly. We extended this example and added the `respond_to?` method in order to conform with Ruby best practices.

Lastly, we looked at a different way to implement metaprogramming with the `define_method` process.

In the next chapter, we're going to walk through the process of working with two of the popular Ruby frameworks—Sinatra and Ruby on Rails.

16
Ruby Web Frameworks

In this chapter, we'll explore the two most popular web frameworks for Ruby programs—Rails and Sinatra—including building applications for both the frameworks. After completing this chapter, you will be able to:

- Explain what a web framework is
- Demonstrate how to build basic Ruby on Rails and Sinatra applications

Sinatra web framework development

Most likely, you're going to be using a web framework to get your Ruby application on the internet. In this section, we are going to talk about a framework called Sinatra (http://www.sinatrarb.com/). This will be an introduction to the framework with the goal of giving you an idea of what this framework is all about and how you can use it to get your Ruby programs on the web.

Sinatra is a framework that is built in Ruby, so it is flexible, fast, and lightweight. Most importantly, it lets you run Ruby code on the web without the need for a lot of Sinatra-specific code.

Let's dive in by creating a couple of files called app.rb and config.ru.

Open the config.ru file and add this code:

```
require './app'
```

This code allows config.ru to pull in the code from the app.rb file.

Let's insert another line of code:

```
run HiSinatra
```

For this code, `HiSinatra` calls a Ruby class that we'll create.

Before going into the code for the `app.rb` file, check whether you have Sinatra installed in your system. Otherwise, type this:

```
gem install sinatra
```

Yes, that's right! Sinatra is simply a Ruby gem (Ruby gems are discussed in `Chapter 14`, *Ruby Gems*); therefore, you need it on your system before you can use it.

Now go to the `app.rb` file and include `sinatra` in it:

```
require 'sinatra'
```

Next, create the `HiSinatra` class:

```
class HiSinatra < Sinatra::Base
  get '/' do
    "Hey Sinatra!"
  end
end
```

In this code, we created a class called `HiSinatra` that inherits from the `Sinatra::Base` class. In this class, we define what we want to show on the home page of the application.

To run the program, start the server with the `rackup` command in your Terminal.

Next, open your browser and go to the localhost address that was shown in the Terminal (it will most likely be `http://localhost:9292`). It should say `Hey Sinatra!`, just like this:

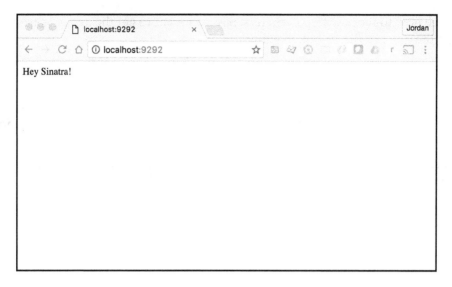

If you type any other URL on your browser for a page you haven't defined, such as
localhost:9292/about, it will throw an error, like this:

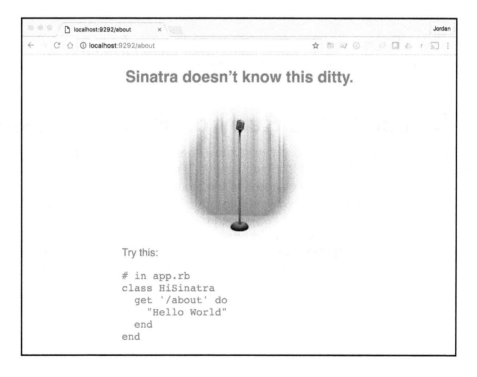

Now let's see how to work with parameters. Say you want to get the age of your user; you can update the `app.rb` file to look like this:

```
get '/:age' do
    "Hi, I'm #{params[:age]} years old."
end
```

If you restart the server, go to the browser, and type `localhost:9292/33`, your message will appear like this:

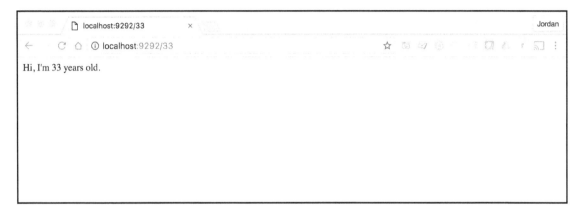

That's how easy it is to get up and running with Sinatra.

Introduction to the Ruby on Rails framework

In this section, we are going to learn how to create a simple Ruby on Rails program. Rails is a popular framework used by many Ruby developers, and I personally have the majority of my Ruby applications built on it. As opposed to the Sinatra (refer to the *Sinatra web framework development* section) framework, which prides itself on being lightweight, Rails has a large number of conventions that you'll need to learn in order to build fully featured applications. In order to learn those conventions and how to build Rails applications, go through these courses: *Learn Rails from Scratch* (`https://rails.devcamp.com/trails/learn-ruby-on-rails-from-scratch`) for basic understanding and the *Rails Code Along* (`https://rails.devcamp.com/trails/rails-bdd-tdd-course`) course for professional Rails development.

Before we go into the code example, ensure you have Rails installed on your system. Like the Sinatra framework, Rails is a Ruby gem, and there are quite a few tutorials that show you how to install Rails. If you need a reference, here is a guide for installing and configuring Rails from the course *Learn Rails from Scratch: Introduction and Installing the Rails Framework* (`https://rails.devcamp.com/trails/learn-ruby-on-rails-from-scratch/campsites/introduction-installing-the-rails-framework`).

To create a new project type, use this command:

```
rails new basic-project
```

This command can build a large number of files for you, such as your config files, tests, assets, and more. Also, it integrates the necessary Ruby gems, such as `json`, `rake`, and `minitest`. It even establishes your database connections.

```
      create  public/favicon.ico
      create  public/robots.txt
      create  test/fixtures
      create  test/fixtures/.keep
      create  test/controllers
      create  test/controllers/.keep
      create  test/mailers
      create  test/mailers/.keep
      create  test/models
      create  test/models/.keep
      create  test/helpers
      create  test/helpers/.keep
      create  test/integration              I
      create  test/integration/.keep
      create  test/test_helper.rb
      create  tmp/cache
      create  tmp/cache/assets
      create  vendor/assets/javascripts
      create  vendor/assets/javascripts/.keep
      create  vendor/assets/stylesheets
      create  vendor/assets/stylesheets/.keep
         run  bundle install
Fetching gem metadata from https://rubygems.org/...........
Fetching additional metadata from https://rubygems.org/..
Resolving dependencies...
Using rake 10.5.0
Using i18n 0.7.0
Using json 1.8.3
Using minitest 5.8.3
Using thread_safe 0.3.5
Using tzinfo 1.2.2
Using activesupport 4.2.5
Using builder 3.2.2
Using erubis 2.7.0
Using mini_portile2 2.0.0
```

Next, let's create our database file and start the Rails server:

```
rake db:create
rake db:migrate
rails s
```

When the server starts, it shows what kind of server and port it is using.

Now, if we go to `localhost:3000`, you can see the welcome page:

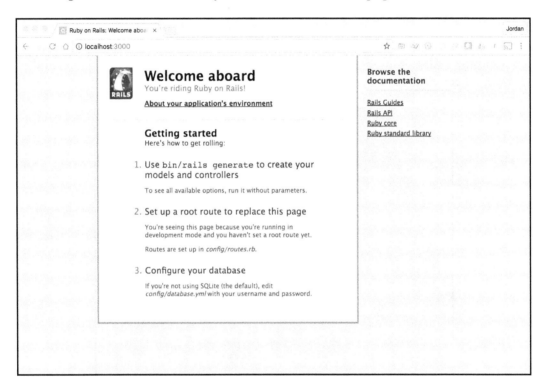

Let's go back to our console and create `scaffold` with the code:

```
rails g scaffold Article title:string body:text
```

This command will create more files for us, such as view template files, a model, controller, database connections, and just about everything else needed for our application.

Also, let's migrate our database because the previous command made more changes to it. To migrate, run the command:

```
rake db:migrate
```

If you go to the application, you will see all the files and folders it created for us. If you open the `schema.rb` file, you will also see that it created a database table for us called `articles` with `title`, `content`, `created_at`, and `updated_at` parameters:

```ruby
# db/schema.rb
ActiveRecord::Schema.define(version: 20160114180152) do

  create_table "articles", force: :cascade do |t|
    t.string   "title"
    t.text     "content"
    t.datetime "created_at", null: false
    t.datetime "updated_at", null: false
  end
end
```

It also created view forms for us that you can see in the `_form.html.erb` file:

```erb
<!-- app/views/articles/_form.html.erb -->

<%= form_for(@article) do |f| %>
  <% if @article.errors.any? %>
    <div id="error_explanation">
      <h2><%= pluralize(@article.errors.count, "error") %>
        prohibited this article from being saved:</h2>
      <ul>
      <% @article.errors.full_messages.each do |message| %>
        <li><%= message %></li>
      <% end %>
      </ul>
    </div>
  <% end %>
  <div class="field">
    <%= f.label :title %><br>
    <%= f.text_field :title %>
  </div>

  <div class="field">
    <%= f.label :body %><br>
    <%= f.text_area :body %>
  </div>
  <div class="actions">
    <%= f.submit %>
  </div>
<% end %>
```

Let's see whether all this works. Start the Rails server with the `rails s` command. Go to `localhost:3000/articles` and it will display this page:

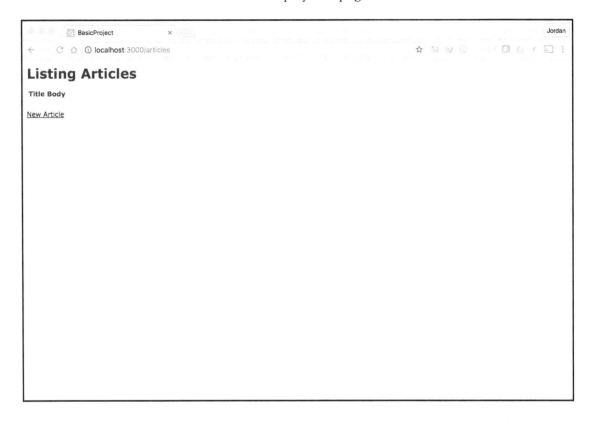

If you click on **New Article**, it will take you to a page where you can enter the title and content:

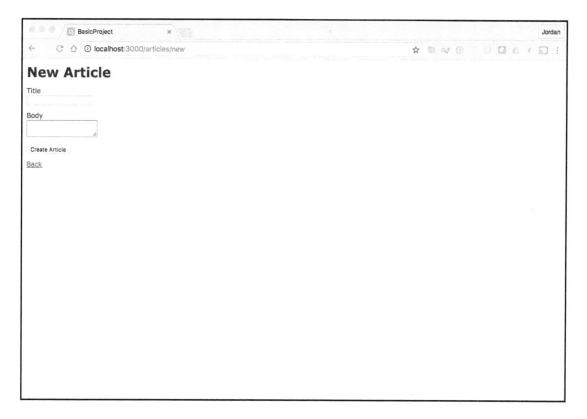

We've been able to create all this functionality without writing a single line of code. Rails is massively more complex than our short introduction and there are libraries of books written on how to build Rails applications. However, this should show you some of the power of the framework and give you ideas for the types of applications you can develop.

Summary

This chapter walked us through how easy it is to get up and running with Sinatra and how it is a great option for building lightweight Ruby programs, such as APIs. We analyzed how to work with a more robust framework and one of the most popular web frameworks in the development community—Ruby on Rails.

In the next chapter, we're going to walk through how to work with APIs in Ruby.

17
Working with APIs in Ruby

Working with external services is a powerful mechanism for building data-driven applications. In this chapter, we'll see how to work with APIs and build a Ruby program that could communicate with a third-party API and parse JSON data. Additionally, you'll be able to:

- Demonstrate how to build an API connector to communicate with external services
- Explain how to pass parameters to an API call
- Apply parsing methods to work with API responses

How to work with APIs in Ruby

This is an exciting section as we are going to discuss how to work with API calls in Ruby. We'll start out with a basic API example and get into more advanced ways of working with APIs in subsequent sections. Refer to the following screenshot:

Here, I have an API called Resty that I built for this course. Resty, short for **RESTful interfaces**, is an API for routing; it's a basic API that has posts and makes them available to the API through the JSON data type, as shown.

Let's discuss a basic way of interacting with this API:

1. Create a file called `apiexample.rb` and open it in the Sublime Text editor.
2. There are many requirements for interacting with APIs in Ruby, and in this section, we are going to leverage the `httparty` Ruby gem to handle API communication. If you don't have this gem on your local system, you can install it with the `gem install httparty` command.
3. Add the `require` code to this file to make `httparty` available to it. The rest of the code looks like this:

```ruby
require 'rubygems'
require 'httparty'

class EdutechionalResty
  include HTTParty
  base_uri "http://edutechional-resty.herokuapp.com"

  def posts
    self.class.get('/posts.json')
  end
end
```

In this code, we created a class called `EdutechionalResty`. We started by including the `HTTParty` call and then used a variable that this gem provides, called `base_uri`. As the name suggests, this is the base URI we are going to use for this application.

Next, we created a method called `posts` and called an instance of this method. It takes a parameter, which is the endpoint of our API's URL. So this is all we have to do inside this class.

4. Now, create an instance of this class and print it out:

```ruby
api = EdutechionalResty.new
puts api.posts
```

If you execute this code, you will see that the output will have the values listed by an external API:

```
{"id"=>1, "title"=>"Test Blog Post",
 "description"=>"Here is the content",
 "url"=>"http://edutechional-resty.herokuapp.com/posts/1.json"}

{"id"=>2, "title"=>"Testing production SMS sending",
 "description"=>"Content for post.",
 "url"=>"http://edutechional-resty.herokuapp.com/posts/2.json"}
```

So this is how you interact with an external API.

How to use the httparty Ruby gem

In the last section, *How to work with APIs in Ruby*, we built a class to call an external API. In this section, we are going to walk through some shortcuts for using the httparty Ruby gem and working with the Stack Overflow API.

Let's start by creating a variable called response and pass a URL to the get method of HTTParty:

```
require 'rubygems'
require 'httparty'
response =
HTTParty.get('http://api.stackexchange.com/2.2/questions?site=stackoverflow
')
```

Now we'll see the different features provided by the built-in HTTParty method.

First, there is the body method that can be called with this code:

```
response.body
```

This will give the following output:

This is the body of all the items available in the Stack Exchange API that we accessed through the `get` method of `HTTParty`. You can see different attributes on every page. You can even copy one of the URLs from the body and check it in the browser.

Now, instead of `body`, let's see what happens when you use a method called `code`:

```
puts response.code
```

If you execute this code, you'll see that it returns a status code of `200`, which means it's working fine.

This method is mainly used to test whether a particular API is working so that you can take actions based on the status value. For example, if the output returns a value of `404`, it means the API does not exist at all, and `500` means there is a problem with the API's server.

Next, let's try another method called `message`. The code for this is:

```
puts response.message
```

Once you run this, you'll get this output—OK.

Next, let's take a look at the API headers with this code:

```
puts response.headers.inspect
```

The output will have all the headers:

```
{"cache-control"=>["private"], "content-type"=>["application/json;
charset=utf-8"], "access-control-allow-origin"=>["*"], "access-control-
allow-methods"=>["GET, POST"], "access-control-allow-
credentials"=>["false"], "x-content-type-options"=>["nosniff"],
"date"=>["Wed, 07 Sep 2016 03:58:01 GMT"], "connection"=>["close"],
"content-length"=>["4997"]}
```

So you can query an entire API and inspect it thoroughly with a few lines of code, which showcases the power and simplicity of the `httparty` gem.

How to create a custom API connector in Ruby

In the *How to use the httparty Ruby gem* section, we walked through the `httparty` Ruby gem segment and we discussed how to integrate built-in classes from the gem to call an API. If you need something more specific, it's a good idea to create a separate class to manage the API processes. That's what we are going to do here while still leveraging some of the key modules supplied by `HTTParty`:

```
require 'rubygems'
require 'httparty'

class StackExchange
  include HTTParty
  base_uri 'api.stackexchange.com'
end
```

In this code, we created a class called `StackExchange`. As the first step, we included the `HTTParty` module so that this class can access the methods provided by the gem. Next, we set `base_uri`, which is the Stack Exchange API URI's path.

Since this is a custom class, let's create an initializer that takes in the arguments `service` and `page`. Inside of the `initialize` method, we will store our API query inside of the `@options` instance variable. Then, inside of `query`, we'll pass in `service` and `page` that we want to be returned:

```
def initialize(service, page)
  @options = { query: {site: service, page: page}}
end
```

Next, we are going to create some additional custom methods. If you remember the previous section, we got a large amount of information when we used the `body` method. To be more specific, we are going to create a method called `questions` that will simply return the questions from Stack Overflow:

```
def questions
    self.class.get('/2.2/questions', @options)
end
```

In this method, we passed a string as the API endpoint. Every web application's documentation provides this endpoint value for you, so you have to look through it to find out what it is. From there, we passed in the query from `options`.

Next, we have a method called `users` that's similar to the `questions` method. This will allow us to query the list of users from Stack Overflow:

```
def users
    self.class.get('/2.2/users', @options)
end
```

Now that we have all our methods, let's create an instance of our class:

```
stack_exchange = StackExchange.new('stackoverflow', 1)
puts stack_exchange.questions
```

In this code, we passed two arguments because our `initialize` method takes two parameters. The first is a service called `stackoverflow`, and we can find information about services in the API's documentation. The second parameter is the page, and we wanted results from only the first page, so we passed in `1`.

Next, we called the `questions` method.

If you execute this code, the output will be as follows:

```
/stackoverflow.com/questions/39365315/error-end-of-script-output-before-headers-while-submiting-html-form-in-python", "title"=>"Er
ror : End of script output before headers while submiting html form in python-cgi"}, {"tags"=>["angularjs", "layout", "printing",
"display"], "owner"=>{"reputation"=>39, "user_id"=>4575981, "user_type"=>"registered", "accept_rate"=>100, "profile_image"=>"https
://graph.facebook.com/1117039348310854/picture?type=large", "display_name"=>"Markus Harthum", "link"=>"http://stackoverflow.com/us
ers/4575981/markus-harthum"}, "is_answered"=>false, "view_count"=>12, "answer_count"=>1, "score"=>0, "last_activity_date"=>1473272
505, "creation_date"=>1473154910, "last_edit_date"=>1473170631, "question_id"=>39345719, "link"=>"http://stackoverflow.com/questio
ns/39345719/create-intelligent-pages-and-columns-layout-in-angular", "title"=>"Create intelligent Pages and Columns Layout in Angu
lar"}, {"tags"=>["mobx", "mobx-react"], "owner"=>{"reputation"=>2622, "user_id"=>1201159, "user_type"=>"registered", "accept_rate"
=>50, "profile_image"=>"https://www.gravatar.com/avatar/e677a583236141e5096e7d3f2d5feb01?s=128&d=identicon&r=PG", "display_name"=>
"cilphex", "link"=>"http://stackoverflow.com/users/1201159/cilphex"}, "is_answered"=>false, "view_count"=>2, "answer_count"=>0, "s
core"=>0, "last_activity_date"=>1473272505, "creation_date"=>1473272505, "question_id"=>39376765, "link"=>"http://stackoverflow.co
m/questions/39376765/cascading-actions-not-rendering", "title"=>"Cascading actions not rendering"}, {"tags"=>["javascript", "angul
arjs"], "owner"=>{"reputation"=>6, "user_id"=>3298156, "user_type"=>"registered", "profile_image"=>"https://www.gravatar.com/avata
r/b3dd548e810330b002617f4b262590af?s=128&d=identicon&r=PG", "display_name"=>"Spencer Sullivan", "link"=>"http://stackoverflow.com/
users/3298156/spencer-sullivan"}, "is_answered"=>false, "view_count"=>21, "closed_date"=>1473230858, "answer_count"=>0, "score"=>-
3, "last_activity_date"=>1473272503, "creation_date"=>1473194269, "last_edit_date"=>1473272503, "question_id"=>39357460, "link"=>"
http://stackoverflow.com/questions/39357460/can-i-return-an-entire-angular-application-as-a-script", "closed_reason"=>"unclear wha
t you&#39;re asking", "title"=>"Can I return an entire angular application as a script?"}, {"tags"=>["c", "arrays"], "owner"=>{"re
putation"=>25, "user_id"=>6719021, "user_type"=>"registered", "profile_image"=>"https://www.gravatar.com/avatar/3269348293683533ab
b2138f87ad7d4e?s=128&d=identicon&r=PG", "display_name"=>"roncook", "link"=>"http://stackoverflow.com/users/6719021/roncook"},
"is_answered"=>false, "view_count"=>27, "closed_date"=>1473272112, "answer_count"=>0, "score"=>-4, "last_activity_date"=>147327250
3, "creation_date"=>1473271724, "last_edit_date"=>1473272503, "question_id"=>39376601, "link"=>"http://stackoverflow.com/questions
/39376601/how-can-i-check-if-an-element-in-an-array-equals-some-value", "closed_reason"=>"off-topic", "title"=>"How can I check if
an element in an array equals some value?"}, {"tags"=>["python", "copy", "argparse"], "owner"=>{"reputation"=>798, "user_id"=>980
818, "user_type"=>"registered", "accept_rate"=>94, "profile_image"=>"https://www.gravatar.com/avatar/4de5157eb76a9869b72c4de85ff77
098?s=128&d=identicon&r=PG", "display_name"=>"Hao Shen", "link"=>"http://stackoverflow.com/users/980818/hao-shen"}, "is_answered"=
>false, "view_count"=>3, "answer_count"=>0, "score"=>0, "last_activity_date"=>1473272500, "creation_date"=>1473272500, "question_i
d"=>39376763, "link"=>"http://stackoverflow.com/questions/39376763/in-python-how-to-deep-copy-the-namespace-obj-args-from-argparse
", "title"=>"In Python, how to deep copy the Namespace obj &quot;args&quot; from argparse"}, {"tags"=>["node.js", "redis", "xmpp",
"mqtt"], "owner"=>{"reputation"=>251, "user_id"=>1404040, "user_type"=>"registered", "accept_rate"=>80, "profile_image"=>"https:/
/www.gravatar.com/avatar/80abb8a8cbc2798c7178ea314f785cdf?s=128&d=identicon&r=PG&f=1", "display_name"=>"vishwas", "link"=>"http://
stackoverflow.com/users/1404040/vishwas"}, "is_answered"=>false, "view_count"=>481, "bounty_amount"=>50, "bounty_closes_date"=>147
3785092, "answer_count"=>0, "score"=>5, "last_activity_date"=>1473272499, "creation_date"=>1440826383, "last_edit_date"=>147327249
9, "question_id"=>32283035, "link"=>"http://stackoverflow.com/questions/32283035/how-do-i-integrate-chat-with-nodejs-and-xmpp-into
-my-existing-web-application", "title"=>"How do I integrate chat with nodejs and xmpp into my existing web application?"}], "has_m
ore"=>true, "quota_max"=>300, "quota_remaining"=>298}
MacBook-Pro-3:ruby-dev admin$
```

If you look through the results, you'll see that the API contains a list of questions and their related URLs. You can copy the `link` attribute and paste it in the browser to check whether it is working. If you access the URL in the browser, you'll see the question returned from the API:

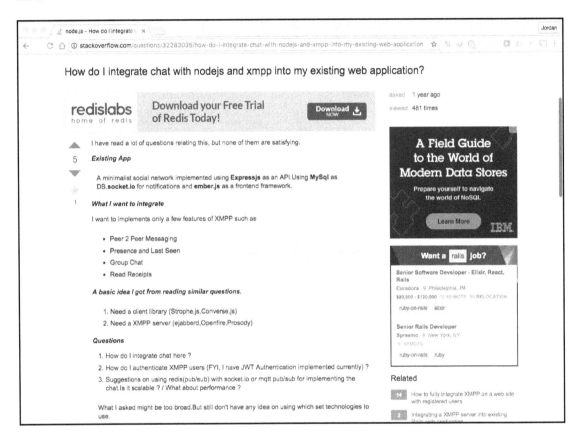

If you go back to the output, you will see other attributes too, such as `title`, `tags`, `owner`, `display_name`, and just about everything else you need to access the Stack Overflow questions.

Let's test whether the `users` method is working by updating the call to the following:

```
stack_exchange = StackExchange.new('stackoverflow', 1)
puts stack_exchange.users
```

If you run the program now, the output will bring up all the users:

```
erator", "user_id"=>13249, "accept_rate"=>100, "location"=>"Winston-Salem, NC", "website_url"=>"http://nickcraver.com/blog/", "lin
k"=>"http://stackoverflow.com/users/13249/nick-craver", "profile_image"=>"https://i.stack.imgur.com/nGCYr.jpg?s=128&g=1", "display
_name"=>"Nick Craver"}, {"badge_counts"=>{"bronze"=>933, "silver"=>572, "gold"=>26}, "account_id"=>237126, "is_employee"=>false, "
last_modified_date"=>1473194380, "last_access_date"=>1473271191, "age"=>45, "reputation_change_year"=>35609, "reputation_change_qu
arter"=>9267, "reputation_change_month"=>1165, "reputation_change_week"=>620, "reputation_change_day"=>121, "reputation"=>425084,
"creation_date"=>1251226343, "user_type"=>"registered", "user_id"=>505088, "accept_rate"=>92, "location"=>"Ulverston, United Kingd
om", "website_url"=>"", "link"=>"http://stackoverflow.com/users/505088/david-heffernan", "profile_image"=>"https://www.gravatar.co
m/avatar/3c0aac2191718ef0309dbc034d9b9961?s=128&d=identicon&r=PG", "display_name"=>"David Heffernan"}, {"badge_counts"=>{"bronze"=
>1709, "silver"=>849, "gold"=>113}, "account_id"=>32093, "is_employee"=>false, "last_modified_date"=>1472241231, "last_access_date
"=>1473272658, "age"=>43, "reputation_change_year"=>38441, "reputation_change_quarter"=>9284, "reputation_change_month"=>828, "rep
utation_change_week"=>389, "reputation_change_day"=>139, "reputation"=>411661, "creation_date"=>1239204526, "user_type"=>"register
ed", "user_id"=>88656, "location"=>"Seattle, WA", "website_url"=>"http://ericlippert.com", "link"=>"http://stackoverflow.com/users
/88656/eric-lippert", "profile_image"=>"https://www.gravatar.com/avatar/6fbdff3ffb6f111d172759b4f05bea0e?s=128&d=identicon&r=PG",
"display_name"=>"Eric Lippert"}, {"badge_counts"=>{"bronze"=>867, "silver"=>766, "gold"=>118}, "account_id"=>9867, "is_employee"=>
false, "last_modified_date"=>1468410457, "last_access_date"=>1473201945, "age"=>43, "reputation_change_year"=>35010, "reputation_c
hange_quarter"=>9231, "reputation_change_month"=>838, "reputation_change_week"=>430, "reputation_change_day"=>120, "reputation"=>4
00766, "creation_date"=>1221783887, "user_type"=>"registered", "user_id"=>18393, "accept_rate"=>82, "location"=>"New York, NY", "w
ebsite_url"=>"http://www.cforcoding.com", "link"=>"http://stackoverflow.com/users/18393/cletus", "profile_image"=>"https://www.gra
vatar.com/avatar/2f364c2e36b52bc80296cbf23da8b231?s=128&d=identicon&r=PG", "display_name"=>"cletus"}, {"badge_counts"=>{"bronze"=>
684, "silver"=>511, "gold"=>30}, "account_id"=>277416, "is_employee"=>false, "last_modified_date"=>1472738535, "last_access_date"=
>1473270680, "age"=>41, "reputation_change_year"=>45708, "reputation_change_quarter"=>11412, "reputation_change_month"=>906, "repu
tation_change_week"=>505, "reputation_change_day"=>175, "reputation"=>395124, "creation_date"=>1294757277, "user_type"=>"registere
d", "user_id"=>571407, "accept_rate"=>100, "location"=>"Saint-Etienne, France", "website_url"=>"http://jnizet.free.fr", "link"=>"h
ttp://stackoverflow.com/users/571407/jb-nizet", "profile_image"=>"https://www.gravatar.com/avatar/2f0d9dec16bae1e06552af55ddefc11f
?s=128&d=identicon&r=PG", "display_name"=>"JB Nizet"}, {"badge_counts"=>{"bronze"=>984, "silver"=>811, "gold"=>75}, "account_id"=>
26957, "is_employee"=>false, "last_modified_date"=>1467748282, "last_access_date"=>1449877865, "age"=>40, "reputation_change_year"
=>33319, "reputation_change_quarter"=>8759, "reputation_change_month"=>878, "reputation_change_week"=>490, "reputation_change_day"
=>200, "reputation"=>393819, "creation_date"=>1235517707, "user_type"=>"registered", "user_id"=>70604, "website_url"=>"http://pasc
al.thivent.name/", "link"=>"http://stackoverflow.com/users/70604/pascal-thivent", "profile_image"=>"https://www.gravatar.com/avata
r/dc1a5b5fdba36ae9cdcf6e267f1a86ca?s=128&d=identicon&r=PG", "display_name"=>"Pascal Thivent"}, {"badge_counts"=>{"bronze"=>1101, "
silver"=>779, "gold"=>36}, "account_id"=>25430, "is_employee"=>false, "last_modified_date"=>1473025456, "last_access_date"=>147320
6345, "age"=>40, "reputation_change_year"=>25247, "reputation_change_quarter"=>6717, "reputation_change_month"=>736, "reputation_c
hange_week"=>361, "reputation_change_day"=>120, "reputation"=>391323, "creation_date"=>1234398071, "user_type"=>"registered", "use
r_id"=>65358, "accept_rate"=>78, "location"=>"Bellingham, WA", "website_url"=>"http://www.reedcopsey.com", "link"=>"http://stackov
erflow.com/users/65358/reed-copsey", "profile_image"=>"https://www.gravatar.com/avatar/87b3a4c585e6fd2ad5308e15e12bdc36?s=128&d=id
enticon&r=PG", "display_name"=>"Reed Copsey"}], "has_more"=>true, "quota_max"=>300, "quota_remaining"=>297}
MacBook-Pro-3:ruby-dev admin$
```

Note that it brings up the list of users on the first page and includes different attributes, such as Gravatar links, `account_id`, `last_accessed_date`, and `last_modified_date`.

So that's how you create a custom API connector in Ruby while using the `httparty` gem.

How to parse an API in Ruby

In our previous sections on APIs, we were able to get the data we wanted from various APIs; however, the data that was returned wasn't very useful. In this section, we are going to learn how to parse the API so that we can get the data we want for further processing.

Let's go back to our `Resty` API and set up the code like this:

```
require 'rubygems'
require 'httparty'

class Resty
  include HTTParty
```

```
    base_uri 'http://edutechional-resty.herokuapp.com'

    def posts
      self.class.get('/posts.json')
    end
  end

  resty = Resty.new
  puts resty.posts
```

In this code, we used the `httparty` gem to call the `Resty` API; we also had a `posts` method to call the endpoint to retrieve the posts. From there, we simply printed out the response from the API. The resulting response will look something like this:

```
{"id"=>1, "title"=>"Test Blog Post", "description"=>"Here is the content",
"url"=>"http://edutechional-resty.herokuapp.com/posts/1.json"}
{"id"=>2, "title"=>"Testing production SMS sending",
"description"=>"Content for post.",
"url"=>"http://edutechional-resty.herokuapp.com/posts/2.json"}
```

To get the individual attributes of this API output, create an `each` block and iterate through it. Also, use the hash syntax to select the `title` items:

```
resty = Resty.new
resty_posts = resty.posts

resty_posts.each do |post|
  puts "Title: #{post['title']}"
end
```

If you execute the code now, you'll have this output:

```
Title: Test Blog Post
Title: Testing production SMS sending
```

We can now continue printing more attributes like this:

```
eductechional_resty.posts.each do |post|
  puts "Title: #{post['title']} | Description: #{post['description']}"
end
```

If you execute the code, you will see the following output:

```
Title: Test Blog Post | Description: Here is the content
Title: Testing production SMS sending | Description: Content for post.
```

So now you know how to successfully parse data coming in from an API. Whenever I find an API that looks intimidating, I have found the best approach is to break it down into small, easy-to-manage chunks, exactly like how we did in this section.

Summary

In summary, we saw how to contact an external API with Ruby. We took a deeper look at how to work with the `httparty` gem and saw how we can query an entire API and inspect it thoroughly with a few lines of code, which showcases the power and simplicity of the `httparty` gem. We also walked through the process of building a custom API connector.

We analyzed how we can query and view raw data from the Stack Overflow API. Additionally, we extended this knowledge and demonstrated how we can parse data in order to use it in a program.

In the next chapter, we're going to walk through popular algorithms and see how to implement them in Ruby.

18
Ruby Algorithms

In this chapter, we're going to put together all of the knowledge that we've gained in this book in order to implement popular algorithms. Specifically, we'll learn how to build advanced algorithms using the Ruby programming language, including sorting methods, such as quick sort and merge sort, along with a number of functional programming algorithms. By the end of this chapter, you will be able to:

- Understand how to build custom algorithms
- Employ both iterative and functional programming techniques to implement algorithms
- Use prime numbers in order to implement various mathematical algorithms

Introduction to sorting algorithms

Welcome to the algorithm section of this course. The next few sections will surely be interesting as we are going to talk about some advanced topics in computer science. These algorithms will help you understand how programming works and give you the tools you'll need to build your own advanced programs.

We'll start out with the sorting algorithms. The reason why we're starting with sorting is because it supplies some of the foundational knowledge that you'll be able to use in more advanced topics, as you'll see as you work through the section.

To explore sorting, let's start by creating an array:

```
a = [1, 5, 1, 2, 10, 100, 3, 1]
```

If you want to sort these values in ascending order, all that you have to do is run:

```
a.sort
```

The output will be `[1, 1, 2, 3, 5, 10, 100]`.

Since this `sort` method works great, there's no real need to create your own `sort` method in Ruby. This brings up the question of why it is important to learn about sorting algorithms when most languages already have sorting mechanisms in place.

There are a number of reasons why it's important to learn about sorting algorithms, but the most critical one is that by creating a sorting algorithm, you'll learn the intricacies of programming in a better way. Sorting algorithms will force you to combine all of the key programming techniques that you've learned through this course, including these topics:

- Working with collections
- Integrating conditionals
- Swapping values inside collections
- Various forms of looping

Let's look at the sorting algorithms we are going to cover in this section—bubble sort, quick sort, and merge sort.

Bubble sort

Bubble sort is an algorithm that we'll learn simply for practice because it's too simple and basic for any real-world use (and incredibly slow). At its core, bubble sort starts from the leftmost value and keeps moving to the right. When moving from left to right, if the next value being compared is greater than the previous one, then it's replaced by a higher value and the sorting continues. In other words, it takes the largest element and bubbles it to the top, and this is why it's called bubble sort. Bubble sort requires many iterations to sort through a typical list since it analyzes one value at a time and finds its right position in the list. In an array of 97 elements, bubble sort would iterate 97 times before it sorts all the values in their right positions.

Quick sort

Quick sort, on the other hand, is a much faster sorting algorithm compared to bubble sort because it uses the concept of **divide and conquer**. This algorithm picks a pivot point and divides the entire list into two groups: one that's below the pivot point and one that's greater than the pivot. It continues to break the collection into smaller and smaller chunks.

It is an efficient algorithm because it sorts values very fast and breaks the entire value set into more manageable pieces. Due to these reasons, quick sort is one of the most widely used sorting algorithm out there, and most people like to use it in their code. Also, the Ruby `sort` method that we used earlier uses the quick sort algorithm to rearrange values.

Merge sort

The last type of sorting algorithm that we'll cover is **merge sort**; this is similar to quick sort, as it uses the divide and conquer method as well. However, merge sort divides the entire collection into subsections; it sorts each subsection and merges it with the next subsection to create a larger group of sorted values.

This type of sorting typically works as well as the quick sort algorithms; however, quick sort is considered as the de facto standard for sorting in most computer science circles.

Implementing the bubble sort algorithm

In this section, we are going to implement the bubble sort algorithm. To recap our sorting algorithm overview, the bubble sort algorithm sorts a collection by moving from left to right, comparing a value with the next value to determine which value is higher (or lower depending on the goal). Typically, it iterates through the entire list many times in order to properly sort a collection. As mentioned in the previous section, bubble sort is not effective for real-world programs because it's too slow.

Bubble sort code example

We'll start off by creating a method called `bubble_sort` that will take `array` as an argument:

```
def bubble_sort(array)
  n = array.length
  loop do
  end
end
```

Next, we assign the length of `array` to a variable called `n`. From there, we create a loop to iterate through the entire array. In this case, we're going to use the generic `loop` mechanism, which operates very much like a `while` loop. Inside `loop`, we check the value of each element and compare it with the next one.

For example, let's say our array contains the following elements: `[1, 4, 1, 3, 4, 1, 3, 3]`. First, bubble sort will compare `1` with `4`; it will do nothing because `1` is smaller. Next, it will check the next two values, which are `4` and `1`, and make them swap because `1` is lesser than `4`. In the next iteration, it will look at `4` and `3` and move `3` to the left. The algorithm will continue this way until the entire array is sorted.

Now let's create a Boolean variable called `swapped` and set it to `false`. This is the variable that will be checked to determine when the program should exit the loop:

```
loop do
  swapped = false
  (n-1).times do |i|
    if array[i] > array[i+1]
      array[i], array[i+1]=array[i+1], array[i]
      swapped = true
    end
  end
end
```

In this code, you'll see that we used a nested iterator that will run `(n - 1)` times. We also used the block variable `i`. Inside this block, we had a conditional to check whether a particular element in the array was greater than the next element, and if greater, we were supposed to swap the elements, which we did. Once that was done, we set the `swapped` variable to `true`. We want to have the loop end when the `swapped` attribute goes through the `(n - 1)` loop and is marked `true`, which would indicate that the array is sorted. In order to implement this sentinel value, we'll add this code to the end of the loop:

```
break if not swapped
```

Lastly, let's return the sorted array back to the user by adding a call to the array at the end of the method.

Let's test this method now with the following code:

```
a = [1, 4, 1, 3, 4, 1, 3, 3]
p bubble_sort(a)
```

The entire code for this method is here:

```
def bubble_sort array
  n = array.length
  loop do
    swapped = false
    (n-1).times do |i|
      if array[i] > array[i+1]
        array[i], array[i+1]=array[i+1], array[i]
        swapped = true
      end
    end
    break if not swapped
  end
  array
end

a = [1, 4, 1, 3, 4, 1, 3, 3]
p bubble_sort(a)
```

If you execute this, you'll get the following output:

```
[1, 1, 1, 3, 3, 3, 4, 4]
```

This means that it's working perfectly and can sort an array.

So now you know how to sort a list of values in Ruby using the bubble sort algorithm.

Implementing the quick sort algorithm

Quick sort is one of the most popular sorting algorithms (see the *Introduction to sorting algorithms* section) to implement, and it is also considered the most efficient in many cases.

Explanation of quick sort

The following visual shows you a high-level view of quick sort:

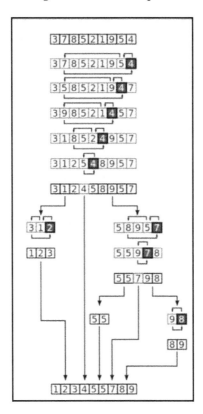

In this example, the algorithm chooses a **pivot value**, which in this case is **4**. From there, it splits the collection into two groups—one with elements to the left of **4** and the other to the right of **4**. Next, quick sort is recursively called on the newly formed left and right collections. For example, the group lower than **4** is chosen next and another pivot point for this subgroup is identified. Based on this pivot point, the array is sorted again. Likewise, the larger group goes through two smaller subgroups, and eventually, all the values are merged together to create a sorted list.

Quick sort code example

Clear as mud? Don't worry if the concept is still a bit fuzzy. Quick sort isn't the most intuitive algorithm if you've never worked with it before. Let's dive into a code example because even though quick sort is quite complex, it actually has a relatively straightforward code implementation if you leverage the right built-in Ruby methods. We'll start by opening up the `Array` class and adding a new method to `Array` called `quicksort`.

An advantage of this metaprogramming approach is that we don't have to pass an argument to the method like we had to in our *Implementing the bubble sort algorithm* section. With this approach, we can directly call the method on any array:

```
class Array
  def quicksort
  end
end
```

Next, let's check whether the array that calls this method is empty, and if so, return an empty array. This is required for both error handling and so that the `quicksort` method will know when to end:

```
def quicksort
  return [] if empty?
end
```

Next, we have to pick our pivot element. Let's say our array is `[34, 2, 1, 5, 3]`; we're going to select a random value as the pivot. To choose this value, implement the following code:

```
pivot = delete_at(rand(size))
```

Essentially, this code picks a random index number from the array's length and passes that random index number to the array to pull out the element at that random index number. This value is stored in a variable called `pivot`.

 By opening up the `Array` class, we are able to call the `size` method without passing it to a specific array because we opened up the `Array` class and `self` is assumed. If you try calling this line of code outside of the `Array` class definition, it would throw an error.

Next, we are going to partition the array based on the `pivot` variable, and to do this, we are going to use the `partition` method. This method splits a collection into two halves. It takes a block as an argument. Inside this block, we're going to use the ampersand syntax to let the program know that it needs to split the array into two components—one that will be less than the pivot value and one that will be greater than the pivot. And, it will store these two collections in variables named `left` and `right`:

```
left, right = partition(&pivot.method(:>))
```

Finally, return the left array, pivot, and the right array and recursively call `quicksort` on both the returned arrays. Use the splat argument represented by * before each collection:

```
return *left.quicksort, pivot, *right.quicksort
```

For our example, let's assume our pivot is 1. The array gets broken down into two parts, and each of these collections will be sorted again using the same method call.

The entire code looks like this:

```
class Array
  def quicksort
    return [] if empty?
    pivot = delete_at(rand(size))
    left, right = partition(&pivot.method(:>))
    return *left.quicksort, pivot, *right.quicksort
  end
end
```

Let's add the code to test this out:

```
arr = [34, 2, 1, 5, 3]
p arr.quicksort
```

The output will be as follows:

```
[1, 2, 3, 5, 34]
```

This means that everything has worked properly. This is one of the shortest implementations of quick sort that I've ever seen. Many other languages have quick sort implementations that would take up hundreds of lines of code; however, by leveraging some built-in Ruby methods, such as `partition`, we were able to consolidate the program and make it easier to read.

Implementing the merge sort algorithm

In this section, we are going to implement the merge sort algorithm. Though merge sort is a popular sorting method, it's not used as much as quick sort because it is slightly slower in real-world scenarios. However, I love merge sort because it is easy to understand from a high-level perspective. In terms of coding, it has a slightly longer code implementation than quick sort but is also easier to understand.

At a higher level, merge sort breaks down the entire array into smaller groups, sorts the values inside each subgroup, and merges it with the larger group to sort a collection.

To implement the algorithm, we are going to create two methods—one called `merge` and the other called `merge_sort`:

```
def merge_sort(list)
end

def merge(left, right)
end
```

As the name suggests, `merge` will take the `right` and `left` values and merge them together. We begin by writing the code inside our `merge` method:

```
def merge(left, right)
  if left.empty?
    right
  elsif right.empty?
    left
  elsif left.first < right.first
    [left.first] + merge(left[1..left.length], right)
  else
    [right.first] + merge(left, right[1..right.length])
  end
end
```

In this `merge` method, we start with a conditional that is expected to return the `right` value if the `left` value is empty and `left` if the `right` is empty. This makes our validation much easier. If both these conditions are not true, then we check whether the first value on the left-hand side is less than the first value on the right-hand side. If so, we recursively call `merge` to bring the arrays together.

Next, we'll implement the `merge_sort` method.

If the length of the array is one item or less, then simply return the array as it requires no sorting. If there are more than two elements in the array, divide the array into two halves. For the left-hand side, recursively call the `merge_sort` method with the parameter being the values from the first to the middle element. For the right-hand side too, call the `merge_sort` method recursively, but the parameters will be the values from the middle to the end of the list. Finally, call the `merge` method with both `left` and `right` arrays as its parameters.

The entire code is as follows:

```
def merge_sort(list)
  if list.length <= 1
    list
  else
    mid = (list.length / 2).floor
    left = merge_sort(list[0..mid - 1])
    right = merge_sort(list[mid..list.length])
    merge(left, right)
  end
end
```

We can test this out with the following code:

```
arr = [4, 1, 5, 1, 33, 312]
p merge_sort(arr)
```

The output of this program is as follows:

```
[1, 1, 4, 5, 33, 312]
```

That's how you implement merge sort in Ruby.

Implementing a prime number counting algorithm

In this section, we are going to create an algorithm that will find all the prime numbers between zero to 2 million. Sound exciting? In traditional programming languages, this algorithm would need hundreds of lines of code, but in Ruby, we're going to see how to implement this efficiently.

To start, let's get access to the `prime` library, and to do this, use this code:

```
require 'prime'
```

Next, store the prime numbers in an array with this code:

```
prime_array = Prime.take_while{ |p| p <2_000_000 }
```

In this code, we created a variable called `prime_array`. In this variable, we store all the prime numbers up to 2 million.

 Ruby ignores underscores with integers, which is how we were able to represent the integer of 2 million with this syntax: 2_000_000. This is helpful when it comes to writing large numbers since we can use underscores instead of commas.

Before we go further, let's print `prime_array` to check whether it's working. If you execute the code, your output will have a huge set of numbers since it has to print every prime number from zero to 2 million:

```
2
3
5
7
11
13
...
1999891
1999957
1999969
1999979
1999993
```

Now if we want to add all the values to our array, we can do it by leveraging the `inject` method:

```
total_count = prime_array.inject{ |sum, x| sum + x }
```

If you print this array and execute the file, the output should be `142913828922`.

The entire code is as follows:

```
require 'prime'

prime_array = Prime.take_while { |p| p <2_000_000 }
total_count = prime_array.inject { |sum, x| sum + x }
puts total_count
```

In this program, we were able to implement a complex math solution with only a few lines of code, using the power of functional programming in Ruby.

How to code the power digit sum algorithm

In this section, we are going to see how to solve a complex math problem that asks us to solve this question—what is the sum of the digits of the number 2 to the 1,000th power?

We can solve this problem with just one line of code in Ruby.

Start by running the equation 2 to the 1,000th power and then convert the value into a string:

```
p (2 ** 1000).to_s
```

If you execute this code, the output will be as follows:

```
"10715086071862673209484250490600018105614048117055336074437503883703510511
24936122493198378815695858127594672917553146825187145285692314043598457757
46985748039345677748242309854210746050623711418779541821530464749835819412673
98767559165543946077062914571196477686542167660429831652624386837205668069
376"
```

This is the value of 2 to the power of 1,000. The next part of the code should add each digit and create a final sum.

First, we want this string to be converted into an array of elements, and the code for this is:

```
p (2 ** 1000).to_s.split(//)
```

If you execute this code, the output will be the same as our string, except now each element will be its own element in an array.

Next, we have to convert everything into an integer again so we can add them together, and we'll use the `map` method to do this:

```
p (2 ** 1000).to_s.split(//).map(&:to_i)
```

The output of this code will be the array:

```
[1, 0, 7, 1, 5, 0, 8, 6, 0, 7, 1, 8, 6, 2, 6, 7, 3, 2, 0, 9, 4, 8, 4, 2, 5,
0, 4, 9, 0, 6, 0, 0, 0, 1, 8, 1, 0, 5, 6, 1, 4, 0, 4, 8, 1, 1, 7, 0, 5, 5,
3, 3, 6, 0, 7, 4, 4, 3, 7, 5, 0, 3, 8, 8, 3, 7, 0, 3, 5, 1, 0, 5, 1, 1, 2,
4, 9, 3, 6, 1, 2, 2, 4, 9, 3, 1, 9, 8, 3, 7, 8, 8, 1, 5, 6, 9, 5, 8, 5, 8,
1, 2, 7, 5, 9, 4, 6, 7, 2, 9, 1, 7, 5, 5, 3, 1, 4, 6, 8, 2, 5, 1, 8, 7, 1,
4, 5, 2, 8, 5, 6, 9, 2, 3, 1, 4, 0, 4, 3, 5, 9, 8, 4, 5, 7, 7, 5, 7, 4, 6,
9, 8, 5, 7, 4, 8, 0, 3, 9, 3, 4, 5, 6, 7, 7, 7, 4, 8, 2, 4, 2, 3, 0, 9, 8,
5, 4, 2, 1, 0, 7, 4, 6, 0, 5, 0, 6, 2, 3, 7, 1, 1, 4, 1, 8, 7, 7, 9, 5, 4,
1, 8, 2, 1, 5, 3, 0, 4, 6, 4, 7, 4, 9, 8, 3, 5, 8, 1, 9, 4, 1, 2, 6, 7, 3,
9, 8, 7, 6, 7, 5, 5, 9, 1, 6, 5, 5, 4, 3, 9, 4, 6, 0, 7, 7, 0, 6, 2, 9, 1,
```

```
4, 5, 7, 1, 1, 9, 6, 4, 7, 7, 6, 8, 6, 5, 4, 2, 1, 6, 7, 6, 6, 0, 4, 2, 9,
8, 3, 1, 6, 5, 2, 6, 2, 4, 3, 8, 6, 8, 3, 7, 2, 0, 5, 6, 6, 8, 0, 6, 9, 3,
7, 6]
```

Lastly, we need to add the array elements together using the `inject` method:

```
p (2 ** 1000).to_s.split(//).map(&:to_i).inject(:+)
```

The final output will be `1366`.

So we were able to solve a challenging problem with a single line of code by leveraging Ruby.

Implementing a humanize counting algorithm

In this section, we are going to solve another complicated math problem using Ruby. The question we'll answer is: If all the numbers from 1 to 1,000 were written out in words, how many letters would be used?

Though this problem looks complex, it can be solved easily in Ruby using the `humanize` library. We start by including the `humanize` gem. If you don't have this gem on your system, install it by running `gem install humanize`.

Now let's dive into the code:

```
require 'humanize'

(1..1000).to_a.map(&:humanize)
```

In the first line, we included the `humanize` gem. On the next line, we built a range from 1 to 1,000 and converted it into an array. Lastly, we called the `humanize` method on this array by utilizing the `map` method. This will convert each element in the array into its named value.

If you execute now, the output will be as follows:

```
["one", "two", "three", "four", "five", "six", "seven", "eight"... "nine
hundred and ninety-six", "nine hundred and ninety-seven", "nine hundred and
ninety-eight", "nine hundred and ninety-nine", "one thousand"]
```

Pretty cool, right? The `humanize` method takes every integer and converts it into words. Without this method, you'd have to write quite a bit of code to get the same output.

Next, we are going to remove all the dashes and spaces by leveraging the little-known `tr` method. The `tr` method is short for **translate** and has some similarities to `gsub`:

```
(1..1000).to_a.map(&:humanize).join.tr(" -", "")
```

In this code, we called the `join` method to convert the array into a giant string. From there, we removed the spaces and dashes by passing them as arguments to the `tr` method.

You can print the string out, and it will look like this:

```
"onetwothreefourfivesixseveneightninetenelevent welve...ninetyeightninehundr
edandninetynineonethousand"
```

Now all we have to do is call the `size` method on our string to get the total number of characters. Running the program will return a value of `21124`, which is the correct answer.

Implementing a date algorithm

In this section, we are going to see how to solve another fun and challenging math problem where we will build an efficient solution to this question—how many Sundays fell on the first of the month during the twentieth century (January 1, 1901, to December 31, 2000)?

To solve this problem, first we have to add the `date` library to our code file. From there, we can set up some variables:

```
require 'date'

start_date = Time.local(1901)
end_date = Time.local(2000,12,31)
sunday_counter = 0
```

The first variable `start_date` has the starting date of the problem. By default, the `local` method starts with January 1 so there is no need to specify the actual day. However, we need to specify the exact date for our `end_date` variable. The third variable `sunday_counter` will count the number of Sundays that fell on the first of the month during the period between `start_date` and `end_date`.

Next, we are going to create a `while` loop:

```
while end_date >= start_date
  if end_date.strftime("%A") == "Sunday" &&
  end_date.strftime("%d") == "01"
    sunday_counter += 1
  end
  end_date -= 86400
end
```

All of the code inside the `while` loop will iterate until the `end_date` is equal to or greater than the `start_date`. Essentially, this loop will count back in time, starting from the `end_date`.

Inside the loop, we converted each timestamp into a string and checked whether it was Sunday and whether it fell on the first day of the month. Because this was the case, we added the `sunday_counter` variable. The `strftime` method converts the date into a string and takes various parameters. Here, the `%A` argument checked for the named day of the week, while `%d` checked for the date of the month.

Finally, we needed to remove a day from the value of `end_date`, and we did that by subtracting the number of seconds in a day, which was `86400`.

Now we can print out the `sunday_counter` value and run the program. You'll see that the output is `171`, and that's the right answer.

The complete code is here:

```
require 'date'

start_date = Time.local(1901)
end_date = Time.local(2000,12,31)
sunday_counter = 0

while end_date>= start_date
  if end_date.strftime("%A") == "Sunday"&&
  end_date.strftime("%d") == "01"
    sunday_counter += 1
  end
  end_date -= 86400
end
puts sunday_counter
```

Working with dates can be confusing. However, when you utilize tools such as `strftime`, you'll discover that dates can be made more manageable.

How to code a Fibonacci digit counter

In this section, we are going to solve another fun math problem that asks us to solve this problem—what is the index of the first term in the Fibonacci sequence to contain 1,000 digits?

In case your college algebra is a little rusty, the **Fibonacci sequence** is a series where you add the next number to the previous number in that series. These numbers can get massive quickly because the addition to the previous value creates a mathematical snowball effect.

Though the problem sounds daunting, it can be solved easily in Ruby.

We are going to start by creating a method called `fibonacci_digit_counter` and define some variables:

```
def fibonacci_digit_counter
  num1, num2, i = -1, 0, 1
end
```

Next, we will create a `while` loop inside of the `fibonacci_digit_counter` method and iterate over the digit value of `i`:

```
while i.to_s.length < 1000
  num1 += 1
  i, num2 = num2, num2 + i
end
```

In this code, we converted the value of `i` into a string and called the `length` method on it, and we wanted the loop to run as long as this length was less than `1000`. Inside the loop, `num1` is the counter that will keep adding the count every time we iterate, and this value is also the final answer to the problem. However, this variable has nothing to do with the Fibonacci number as that is managed by the variables `i` and `num2`.

Also, note that we set the value of `i` to `num2` and `num2` to the sum of `num2` and `i`. This is exactly how the Fibonacci series is calculated.

Finally, we returned the variable `num1` and printed the `fibonacci_digit_counter` method.

If you run the program, the output will be `4782`, which is the correct answer.

The full code is as follows:

```
def fibonacci_digit_counter
  num1, num2, i = -1, 0, 1
  while i.to_s.length < 1000
    num1 += 1
    i, num2 = num2, num2 + i
  end
  num1
end
p fibonacci_digit_counter
```

Implementing a permutation algorithm

In this section, we are going to build an algorithm that is going to leverage a number of powerful Ruby methods. The math problem that we are going to solve is a problem that asks this—what is the millionth lexicographic permutation of the digits 0, 1, 2, 3, 4, 5, 6, 7, 8, and 9?

This may seem like an intimidating problem, but thankfully, it can be solved quickly with Ruby, thanks to some functional programming methods.

So what is a **lexicographic permutation**? It's the number of permutations you can make with a given set of numbers. For example, there are six different numbers you can create with the digits 0, 1, and 2.

Now that we know how to build a permutation for three numbers, we have to find the millionth permutation of the digits 0 to 9.

In Ruby, we can do this with a single line of code:

```
p [0,1,2,3,4,5,6,7,8,9].permutation.to_a[999_999].join
```

In this code, we created an array of numbers from 0 to 9 and called the method `permutation` on it.

From there, we converted the `permutation` object into an array by calling the `to_a` method on it.

Next, we called the 1,000th variable in the array. If you remember, an array index starts at 0, so the 1,000th variable has an index value of 999,999. Instead of a comma, I used the _ symbol for better readability.

Finally, we called the `join` method to convert the array into a string.

If this still seems a bit fuzzy, let's see how the `permutation` method works in the `irb` console. Execute this code:

```
arr = [1, 2, 3]
arr.permutation { |i| p i }
```

Its output will be as follows:

```
[1, 2, 3]
[1, 3, 2]
[2, 1, 3]
[2, 3, 1]
[3, 1, 2]
[3, 2, 1]
```

So the `permutation` method takes care of building all the combinations for us and even gives us the lexicographic representation.

Now, if you execute the file, the output will be `2783915460`, and that's the right answer.

Implementing an amicable number algorithm

In this section, we are going to find a solution in Ruby for the math problem that asks this—evaluate the sum of all the amicable numbers under 10,000.

So that made perfect sense, right? In case your amicable number knowledge is a little rusty like mine was, let's look at a definition of **amicable numbers**:

Let $d(n)$ be defined as the sum of proper divisors of n (numbers less than n that could be divided evenly into n). If $d(a) = b$ and $d(b) = a$, where $a \neq b$, then a and b are an amicable pair, and both a and b are called amicable numbers.

Still unclear? The following is the full explanation:

Essentially, you take a number, identify all its divisors, and add them together to get a value. Next, take that final sum value, identify its divisors, and add them together. If this second sum value is the same as the original number for which you found divisors in the first place, then both the original number and its final sum are considered amicable numbers.

The question is asking us to find the sum of all such amicable numbers under 10,000.

Now we are going to solve this problem in Ruby. We are going to include a gem called `mathn` and then do some metaprogramming by opening the `Integer` class. Inside this class, let's create a new method called `dsum`:

```
require 'mathn'

class Integer
  def dsum
    return 1 if self < 2
    pd = prime_division.flat_map{|n,p| [n] * p}
    ([1] + (1...pd.size).flat_map{ |e| pd.combination(e).map{
    |f| f.reduce(:*)
    }}).uniq.inject(:+)
  end
end
```

We returned the value of 1 as the object value was less than 2. This makes sense because 1 has no divisor besides itself.

Next, we created a variable called `pd` to store the result of our prime division calculation. For this, we called a method called `flat_map` that takes two parameters—one being n and the other being p.

Inside this block, we created a block that gave us all the prime divisors that were provided.

Next, we had a complicated line that summed all the prime divisors. Let's go over each part of that line.

In the first part, we combined all the prime divisors' values and added 1 to that array. This combines all the prime divisors, including 1, into a single array. Then we once again called the `flat_map` method and passed a nested block to it. Inside this block, we called a method called `combination` to find all the combinations in our prime divisors and then pass the multiplication method to each element and create a product. At the end of the line, we called the `uniq` method since we only wanted to grab unique matches. Finally, `inject` returned the sum of all the values.

Next, we are going to create another method called `find_d_sum` that will call this `dsum` method. We'll call this method from the outside, where we opened up the `Integer` class:

```
def find_d_sum(n)
  n.times.inject do |sum, cur|
    other = cur.dsum
    (cur  != other && other.dsum == cur) ? sum + cur :sum
  end
end
```

The first line iterates over each of the numbers n times provided by the method argument and it leverages the `inject` method to combine the values. The second line stores that value in a variable called `other`. Next is a conditional that checks whether `cur` is not equal to the `other` and also whether the `dsum` value of `other` is equal to `cur`. If that's true, we print the value of `sum` and `cur`. Otherwise, we return only the value of `sum`.

Finally, we print the value returned by `find_d_sum`.

If you execute the code, the output will be `31626`, and that's the right answer.

Since this is complicated, play around with this code and see what the effect is when you change isolated components and how that affects the final output. Also, explore some of these methods that are new to you.

Implementing a factorial algorithm

Another interesting problem that we are going to tackle is how to calculate the factorial digit sum. In this program, we need to solve this—find the sum of the digits in the number 100.

This is a perfect problem to build a solution for because it combines a number of topics that we have learned in this Ruby programming course. I would even suggest you try building the program yourself before we head to the solution as this will give you a hands-on feel of Ruby algorithm development. You have all the knowledge needed to build it.

If you get stuck, don't worry! We will still build it together.

If you're new to factorials, the question is self-explanatory. A **factorial** is a number that is the multiplied value of itself as well as all the digits up to 1. Factorials can get quite massive in a short period of time because they are a compounded multiple of a range of numbers. The sum of the individual digits of a factorial is the factorial digit sum. In this problem, we have to find the factorial digit sum of 100.

We are going to start by creating a method called `factorial_value_sum_generator`:

```
def factorial_value_sum_generator(factorial)
  arr = (1..factorial).to_a.reverse.each {
  |i| factorial += factorial * (i - 1)}
  factorial.to_s.split(//).map(&:to_i).inject(:+)
end
p factorial_value_sum_generator(100)
```

In this method, we sent the `factorial` as an argument. In the code, we created an array and converted all the values from `1` to the `factorial` argument into an array. After that, we reversed this array because we wanted to multiply each value, starting from the `factorial` argument value all the way to `1`.

Next, we iterated through the array with the variable `i`. Then, we add the product of the factorial and the value after it to the factorial. For example, if we have an array `[10,9,8,7...1]`, then our code will multiply `10` with `9`, that's `i-1`. The program will then add it to the factorial value to give a total value of `19` during the first iteration.

Once that is done, we sum up the digits, and this was done in the next line where we converted the `factorial` value into a string and called the `split` method on it. Next, we called the `map` method and passed the integer value as its argument. Finally, we called the `inject` method to add up all the values.

At the end, we printed out the value returned by our method.

If you run the program, the output will be `648`, and that's correct!

Implementing an even Fibonacci number algorithm

In this section, we are going to solve a mathematical challenge that asks us to find even Fibonacci numbers. The full question is—by considering the terms in the Fibonacci sequence whose values do not exceed 4 million, find the sum of the even-valued terms.

Since this is a fairly straightforward problem (assuming that you are familiar with the Fibonacci sequence), we're going to build a more exhaustive solution to further our understanding of Ruby. We're not going to write a one-line code answer for this problem; rather, we are going to build a class:

```ruby
class Fibbing
  def initialize(max)
    @num_1 = 0
    @i = 0
    @sum = 0
    @num_2 = 1
    @max = max
  end
  def even_fibonacci
    while @i<= @max
      @i = @num_1 + @num_2
```

```
        @sum += @i if@i % 2 == 0
        @num_1 = @num_2
        @num_2 = @i
      end
    @sum
  end
end
```

In this code, we created a class that has an `initialize` method. The `initialize` method defines a number of variables inside it. Next, we created a method called `even_fibonacci`. In this method, we have a `while` loop that runs as long as the value of i is greater than the value of max. From there, we added the value of `num1` and `num2` to i.

In the next line, we added the value of i to the sum, but we do this only if i is even. Lastly, we set the value of `num_1` to `num_2` and `num_2` to the iterator variable i since this is how Fibonacci numbers are calculated. We make this entire method return the value of the `sum`.

Next, let's create an instance of the class and pass the max parameter to it:

```
result = Fibbing.new(4_000_000)
p result.even_fibonacci
```

The final output will be `4613732`, which is correct.

Implementing the least common multiple

In this section, we are going to solve a math problem that asks—what is the smallest positive number that is evenly divisible by all the numbers from 1 to 20?

Ruby really shines when it comes to answering questions such as these. In fact, the entire solution to this problem is shown as follows:

```
p (1...20).to_a.reduce(:lcm)
```

In this code, we converted a range of numbers from 1 to 20 into an array. On this array, we called the `reduce` method and passed the built-in `lcm` method. The `lcm` method will get the least common multiple of the value passed to it.

If you execute this code, the answer will be `232792560`, which is the right solution.

This code illustrates the power of functional methods and how they can make coding a much easier and more enjoyable experience in Ruby.

Summary

We saw how to implement all three types of sorting algorithms—the bubble sort, the quick sort, and the merge sort. Understanding these sorting methods can be quite handy when learning a new concept, sitting an exam, or going through a coding interview.

We walked through a program that counts prime numbers with only a few lines of code using the power of functional programming combined with the `prime` number library in Ruby. We saw how to build a power digit sum algorithm. We analyzed how to leverage the `humanize` gem in order to convert integers into words. This is a powerful tool that you can utilize in a number of real-world programs. We also demonstrated the power of the `map` method and how it can be utilized to iterate and alter the values in a collection. We also saw how to work with dates in a Ruby program.

We walked through how to build a Fibonacci sequence and then query specific values. This is especially helpful when developing programs that create dynamic sets of data that need to be searched through. We extended our knowledge of collections by working through the permutation method in Ruby.

In the next section, we worked with the amicable number algorithm, which was not an easy program to build. We walked through the process of building a factorial algorithm and saw how to manipulate arrays, map over values, and sum collections to produce the intended result. Lastly, we looked at a different approach to implementing a Fibonacci equation. We also built the least common multiple program in Ruby. In the next chapter, we'll look at how to work with machine learning algorithms in Ruby.

19
Machine Learning

One of the fastest growing sectors in development is machine learning. In this chapter, you will learn how to integrate machine learning algorithms into a Ruby program, including how to build a decision tree, train it, and have it output dynamic results. By the end of this chapter, you will be able to:

- Demonstrate how to implement machine learning algorithms in Ruby
- Use the decision tree code library to build a learning algorithm

Big data analysis

In this section, we are going to walk through the exciting topic of big data analysis. At a high level, big data analysis is the process that helps build algorithms that can analyze vast amounts of data and allows you to generate behavior-based decisions from that data.

For big data analysis in this section, we'll be using the decision tree gem. It uses the ID3 algorithm and is very efficient in taking data and making decisions based on it:

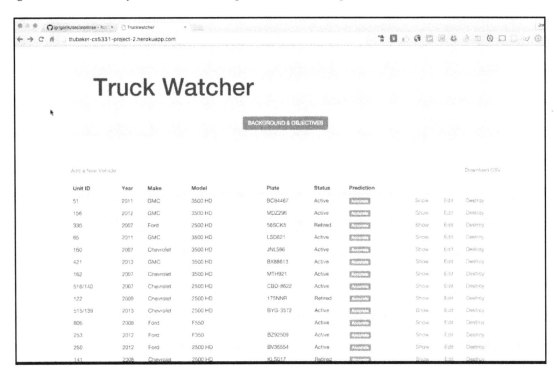

I'd like to show you a practical big data project I built for a client about a year ago. This was a large company that had more than a thousand trucks and they wanted an application that showed when each truck should retire based on historical data. For years, the company had been forced to make arbitrary decisions based on gut feelings. An application like this would allow for more informed, data-driven decisions.

This application took in all of the company's data, such as model, make, year, mileage, maintenance, and other pertinent factors and used an algorithm that generated a recommendation for when a particular truck should be retired.

86	2008	Chevrolet	2500 HD	30GPP7	Active	Accurate	Show	Edit	Destroy
308	2010	Chevrolet	1500	76D6301	Active	Accurate	Show	Edit	Destroy
235	2012	GMC	3500 HD	BX48969	Active	Accurate	Show	Edit	Destroy
317	2008	Chevrolet	2500 HD	07YHZ6	Active	Accurate	Show	Edit	Destroy
76	2006	Chevrolet	1500	29CBR4	Active	Accurate	Show	Edit	Destroy
61	2009	Chevrolet	3500 HD	5786AP	Active	Accurate	Show	Edit	Destroy
80	2009	Chevrolet	2500 HD	AJ47557	Retired	Accurate	Show	Edit	Destroy
151	2007	Chevrolet	1500	JJJ929	Retired	Accurate	Show	Edit	Destroy
23	2008	Chevrolet	3500 HD	28PDS8	Retired	Accurate	Show	Edit	Destroy
101	2011	Chevrolet	2500 HD	B880856	Active	Accurate	Show	Edit	Destroy
278	2010	Ford	2500 HD	AK71548	Active	Accurate	Show	Edit	Destroy
21	2007	Chevrolet	1500	09LBP7	Active	Accurate	Show	Edit	Destroy
228	2012	Chevrolet	2500 HD	MDZ298	Active	Accurate	Show	Edit	Destroy
342	2008	Ford	F-250 Super Duty	88ZHD8	Active	Accurate	Show	Edit	Destroy
138	2008	Chevrolet	2500 HD	KJB451	Retired	Accurate	Show	Edit	Destroy
20	2010	Chevrolet	2500 HD	AJ62783	Active	Needs Attention	Show	Edit	Destroy
345	2008	Chevrolet	1500	MSA944	Retired	Accurate	Show	Edit	Destroy
334	2008	Ford	2500 HD	947RLR	Active	Accurate	Show	Edit	Destroy
198	2008	Chevrolet	1500	KJK061	Active	Accurate	Show	Edit	Destroy
359	2008	Ford	2500 HD	11LDK7	Retired	Accurate	Show	Edit	Destroy

These are some of the factors that the algorithm took into consideration to decide whether a particular truck should retire or not:

```
Unit: 20

Year: 2010

Make: Chevrolet

Model: 2500 HD

Plate: AJ62783

Mileage: 121056

Vin: 1GC5KVBG6AZ247592

Category: Service

Color: White

Status: Active

Equipment: 20 - 2010 Chevrolet 2500

Fuel: Gasoline

Weight:

Transmission: Automatic

Custom: 14ST20

Purchase code:

Purchase price: 30899.0

Start cost: 30899.0

Virtual meter: 121056

Repairs: 3

Services: 13
```

In this section, we will walk through a number of ways in which we can build big data applications using Ruby.

Basic decision tree implementation

This is a simple introduction to setting up a decision tree in Ruby. We'll start off with a simple setup. In this section, we're going to build a medical analysis tool. In order to follow along, make sure that you've installed the `decisiontree` Ruby gem. If you don't have it on your system, you can install it by running:

```
gem install decisiontree
```

To start building a decision tree, let's create a basic application. Begin by pulling in the required gem libraries:

```
require 'rubygems'
require 'decisiontree'
```

Addition of attributes

The next step is to include a single attribute called `Temp`. This attribute will indicate the temperatures of individuals in the database and whether they are sick or healthy. This will give us the tool to decide which person is sick and which one is not:

```
attributes = ['Temp']
```

Addition of training data and its values

Now we are going to introduce training data, which is the data that the machine learning algorithm will learn from. This will contain information about what data we are going to be analyzing with our decision tree program. The code will look like this:

```
training = [
]
```

Next, we are going to load some basic data into our `training` array in order to provide it with values to analyze. We're going to place values in the array that would fit our requirements. For example, `98.7` is healthy, `99.1` is still healthy, `99.5` starts getting a little bit sick, `100.5` is crazy sick, and `107.5` results in a dead patient. Enter the values in the training program in this format:

```
training = [
  [98.7, 'healthy'],
  [99.1, 'healthy'],
  [99.5, 'sick'],
  [100.5, 'sick'],
  [102.5, 'crazy sick'],
  [107.5, 'dead'],
]
```

Calling the ID3 method

Now with the training function loaded with data, our next step should be to create the decision tree itself. We can do this by calling on the modules provided by the decision tree library and passing in the module that we want to use. We're going to leverage the ID3 algorithm for this example. The ID3 tree is a popular decision-making algorithm, which will give us access to its functions.

After calling the ID3 algorithm, we need to instantiate a new decision tree and pass in the first argument, which is `attributes`. With this, we pass in the training data and the default will be set as `sick`. All of this will be set to `:continuous`, which indicates that we are setting the decision tree to run continuously. Your decision tree instantiation should look like this:

```
dec_tree = DecisionTree::ID3Tree.new(attributes, training, 'sick',
:continuous)
```

Now we introduce the `train` method, which is designed to train the decision tree knowledge engine. The function of this method is to take in all the values and their respective results:

```
dec_tree.train
```

Function of the train method

Now let's add another attribute called `Name` (which is silly, since someone's name won't determine whether they're sick or not, but I'm going to use it for the sake of the example). Next, add names to the training data:

```
attributes = ['Temp' , 'Name']
training = [
  [98.7, 'jordan' , 'healthy'],
  [99.1, 'tiffany' , 'healthy'],
  [99.5, 'sick'],
  [100.5, 'sick'],
  [102.5, 'crazy sick'],
  [107.5, 'dead'],
]
```

Addition of the test method

Now that we have the training data in order, we can add the data we actually want to test. Let's add a line of code that looks like this:

```
test = [98.7, 'healthy']
```

The `healthy` part is included just to test the algorithm. In a real-world application, we wouldn't know whether the patient is healthy; that's what the program will determine.

Setting up decision variables

Next, we're going to utilize the `predict` method and pass in the test data. We will call our decision tree, which has been trained with our historical data, and we will call `predict`, which is a built-in method that the decision tree gem provides. This will allow us to pass in the argument of the test data and compare it with the data it's been compared against, then it will give us a prediction. The code will look like this:

```
decision = dec_tree.predict(test)
```

Print the results out

Now we are going to create two `puts` statements that will print the data. `Prediction` is assigned for the decision, and `Reality` will ensure that our algorithm is working properly:

```
puts "Prediction: #{decision}"
puts "Reality: #{test.last}"
```

Testing the program

Let's run the program and see whether it works or not. If we use the information provided, it will print out `healthy`, which means that our base case is working properly. You can test another example by setting the `test` array to a temperature of `107.5`, and the result will be this—`dead`.

Advantage of decision trees over if...else statements

You must be wondering why we chose a decision tree instead of `if...else` statements. The `if...else` statements are great for a small amount of data. But when you have to design a big data module in real-life scenarios (such as with hospital data), there will be millions of data points and `if...else` statements would not be practical. You need something more robust, such as a decision tree, in order to analyze a large amount of data.

How to develop a big data analysis application in Ruby

In this section, we are going to work on a big data classification algorithm, based on a decision tree algorithm that you can use in a real-world scenario.

Let's say you're working for a company and want to find out your ideal market. You also want to know who are the customers buying your product or service. To answer these questions, you can leverage the vast amounts of data you have collected from historical customers.

As with the previous lesson, let's call our `rubygems` and `decisiontree` code libraries and set up some attributes. In this example, our attributes will be demographic data, such as age, education, income, and marital status. We also have some training data that will be used by the decision tree to make decisions:

```
require 'rubygems'
require 'decisiontree'

attributes = ['Age', 'Education', 'Income', 'Marital Status']
training = [
  ['36-55', 'Masters', 'High', 'Single', 1],
  ['18-35', 'High School', 'Low', 'Single', 0],
  ['36-55', 'Masters', 'High', 'Single', 1],
  ['18-35', 'PhD', 'Low', 'Married', 1],
  ['< 18', 'High School', 'Low', 'Single', 1],
  ['55+', 'High School', 'High', 'Married', 0],
  ['55+', 'High School', 'High', 'Married', 1],
  ['55+', 'High School', 'High', 'Married', 1],
  ['55+', 'High School', 'High', 'Married', 1],
  ['< 18', 'Masters', 'Low', 'Single', 0],
]
```

In the training data, the last value of 1 or 0 denotes whether each person is a customer or not, where 1 indicates the person is a customer and 0 otherwise. The preceding data is just an example, as you'll have thousands of such data points in the real world. In fact, the more data you have, the better your decision tree will be. If you have millions of data points, then you can drill down with more precision to get the information you want.

Typically, you can get all this type of data through the company's CRM software.

Next, let's instantiate our decision tree:

```
dec_tree = DecisionTree::ID3Tree.new(attributes, training, 1, :discrete)
dec_tree.train
```

In this code, we passed attributes and training data. The default value is 1 and the algorithm is going to be `discrete`. We also have to train the decision tree with the `train` method.

Now we can test some values to see how our system works:

```
test = ['< 18', 'High School', 'Low', 'Single']
decision = dec_tree.predict(test)
puts "Predicted : #{decision}"
```

The output is as follows:

```
Predicted : 1
```

It predicted that this person should be a customer. The attributes we tested match one of the records in training data, and this is why the decision tree was able to predict that this person is a customer.

Next, let's change the income level of test data, such as:

```
test = ['< 18', 'High School', 'High', 'Single']
```

If you run, the decision tree still says this person should be a customer, which is the right answer.

Let's change the test data a little bit again:

```
test = ['18-35', 'High School', 'Low', 'Married']
```

The output says this person should not be a customer. If you're a company, then you may not want to spend a lot of money on marketing to this person because they do not seem to be interested in what you're offering (at least on a historical basis).

This is how you implement a big data analysis module in Ruby to allow you to make some advanced decisions.

Summary

This chapter walked us through a practical implementation of machine learning in Ruby. It also showed a number of ways in which we can build machine learning applications.

We looked at how to leverage the decision tree library in order to train a program via historical data and then let the program make an informed recommendation. We analyzed how to extend our decision tree knowledge to build a more complex machine learning algorithm.

We reviewed how to leverage machine learning in order to build out a complex recommendation engine. This type of tool can be utilized in real-world applications to help an organization make informed decisions based on historical data.

Index